MEMOIR OF A MUSICAN

by

Dr. Jack Normain Kimmell

chapters in this book:

Bloomsburg and Early Youthful Days
The Poconos and Those Glorious Days
New York Military Academy
Bucknell University
Wills Eye Hospital
Music on the Road and Johnny Mehegan
Julius Hartt Music School and Hartford
I'm In the Army Now!
Midland, Michigan State University and Marriage
Married Life and the "Big Apple"
Grand Rapids and Short New York Visit
Return to Grand Rapids and Summer Stock
Richmond and Re-Saugatuck
Return to the Big Apple and Mary Stiles
Massachusetts and Marriage #2
Welcome to Arizona
Europe
Home, Owen and Stuff
Re-Grand Rapids and more Composing
Family and Grand Children

Prologue

One hot summer day, in the late nineteen eighties in Scottsdale, Arizona, while skinny dipping in our swimming pool and casually musing about my life, a head suddenly appeared over our wall. It moved back and forth, looked at me, shook and snorted "feed me!" I climbed out of the pool, grabbed some shorts, opened up the wall gate, and headed across a large dirt arena to our "Porta Barn." I felt an impatient something nudging my rear, pushing me from behind like a Border Collie pushes a sheep. It was the nose of my daughter Kathy's magnificent horse "Midnight." I felt needed. He wanted to be fed and that made me feel real important. He knew I'd gotten his message because suddenly he galloped like thunder across the arena and into his stall. I followed, threw a leaf of hay into his food bin and watched the huge, beautiful, amazing animal chomp away, staring at me with his wild eyes. For a moment I had this wonderful feeling of contentment. Yet there I was in hot, "foreign" Arizona, a musician/composer in the midst of the desert with my wife Mary, a daughter, two cats, two dogs and a horse. Since I'd spent most of my life in the East and Midwest, what the hell was I doing here? I thought of the years gone by. Gone by and gone by! And how many "gone byes" could my memory conjure up well enough to translate into words to be read? Who, besides me, would read them anyway? There's no doubt that some memories would be painful during this trip through nostalgia land...even the good ones.

As this was begun a number of years ago in Arizona, "life" got in the way and. now, living in Michigan, I came across this on a floppy disc and decided to correct, embellish and continue these "Memoirs of a Musician" for who so ever cares to take the time to read.

A good writer should have excellent writing skills, a substantial vocabulary, a creative imagination, a decent outlook on life and be well read and probably should also have an objective, broad, questioning outlook on life. I do have a

4

questioning outlook on life but I doubt if the rest is me. Also back in Michigan, in the midst of one of our heated arguments in front of people who sometimes think I'm great, Adrian Swets, one of my best friends, proclaimed in an unusually loud voice, "You're not philosophical!" Although that possibility was staring me in the face there are a few things I have going for me: I'm persistent and competitive as a bull dog, have a favorable amount of brains and imagination and have damn good software.

But where do I begin? Probably at the beginning but I know it won't be any great literary epic. However, maybe I'll be inspired to recall memorable times of my life along with those not worthy of remembering. And some day, if she or he had nothing else to do, it might be picked up and read. It's impossible to remember, at least earlier events in some kind of exact chronological order, but I'll try my best and begin back in my early days in Bloomsburg, Pennsylvania and that's a *lonnnggg* way back

Bloomsburg and Early Youthful Days

Bloomsburg, described often as "a little town nestled in the Susquehanna Valley" is, as Bloomsburgers would say, where I was, "brung up." It's up about eighty miles from Harrisburg on one branch of the Susquehanna River, and down another sixty-four miles on another branch from Wilkes Barre. Back in the forties population was about 10,000. When my brother Bobby and I moved away it was probably 9,998. Bloomsburgers boasted that their little town was the only "Incorporated town in Pennsylvania." I never understood what that meant but for anyone who's interested, an incorporated town, in the United States is: *"an incorporated municipality, that is, one with a charter received from the state similar to a city. An incorporated town will have elected officials, as differentiated from an unincorporated community, which exists only by tradition and does not have elected officials at the town level."* And blah blah blah. I still don't understand! How Bloomsburg got its name is a question I've heard with several answers. Some say it was named after Samuel Bloom, others claim it was named after its "blooming" laurel trees, still others swear that some of the early settlers from Bloomsbury, New Jersey named the town. Take your pick!

Bloomsburg is the County Seat of Columbia County and in the center, on Market and Main, sits the old City Hall Building confronted by a large fountain surrounded by flowers. And of course the most important street in town is called "Main Street," which runs east and west and a rather small street named "Center Street" separates east from west. Other streets have rather complicated names like East Street, Iron, Fountain, Market, Jefferson, Railroad, Fourth, Third, etc...not too easy to get lost. On one side of the Susquehanna, the last time I heard, there is there's an airport for small airplanes called Bloomsburg Municipal Airport. If you look down from a steep hill in any part of town you can see it. On the other side of the river the smooth green mountains, part of the Appalachians, still rise up just high enough to remind you they're always

8

there. It's really quite a beautiful little town. That is except when there's a flood which they've had several times.

A lovely rather old college sits on top of the steep hill at the eastern end of Main Street and looking up, from anywhere in town, you can see the shiny, white round dome of the main building saying "come on up". The college, through the years has gone through several name changes. First it was Bloomsburg Normal School, and then Bloomsburg State Teachers College, and now, since it's grown so much, in July 1983, became Bloomsburg University of Pennsylvania. In the early days a private grammar school, in order to give its students the advantage of a teaching experience, was part of the college. Another function was to give so called "mentally sharp," more advanced kids a specialized education different from that of a typical primary public school. I guess that must have included my brother Bobby and me.

We first lived at 25 East Fifth Street, at the lower end of town in a small building attached to a fire department in those days called a "hose house." Our apartment, of Andrew Filson Kimmel and family, on the second floor, consisted of a small living room, two bedrooms and a bathroom. You can imagine the furniture! We weren't poor but sometimes were teetering on its edge. The first floor consisted of A.F.'s radio and refrigerator shop and workshop and a kitchen in the rear. Our telephone number was 275. Can imagine how long ago that was?

Grammar school meant trudging up a long, paved, steep hill to the college, twice a day, once in the morning, and again at noon for lunch. *No school cafeterias in those days*. The hill was steep enough to give this "brat" this big challenge:

One day I decided to climb into my little red wagon and ride, like a bat out of hell, down that hill. There was hardly ever any traffic on the cross streets so no worry here! Resting on my knees in my wagon, while some of my friends watched with mouths open wide in awe and fear, I went roaring down, picking up speed, faster and faster. Suddenly, oh crap, out zoomed a car from

Third Street. Panicking, I swerved, crashed into a ditch landing on one knee and cutting it on some stones. I looked stupid and my knee was looking serious, because pieces of leaves and dirt were inside and it was bleeding like a stuck pig. The gang of scared of kids ran down, picked me up and pulled me, wailing loud and clear, home in my wagon. My furious mother carted me off to the doctor who, as he stitched me up said, "Boys will be boys!" My mother loved that! I have a nasty scar that never affected my knee but gave me something to show the kids. One of my juvenile favorites was this:

If my dad had a large cardboard box from some unpacked appliance, I'd haul it outside on the lawn and pretend it was an airplane. After cutting holes in the front for windows and making some kind of contraption for the "controls," I'd sit inside, wearing a goggled helmet, pretending I was a heroic fighter pilot like Cagney or Errol Flynn. For hours I'd brummm and hum and bounce around inside, rat-rat-tatting on make believe machine guns. Then all at once "wham!"

Over I'd go in the box, "crashing" and sprawling out onto the grass. "Boys will be boys!"

There were summers when my mother (I never called her "mom") would help my brother and me set up a lemon or orange aid stand on the sidewalk in front of our building. (Maybe it was because we never had an allowance.) Patiently we'd wait for the kids in the neighborhood to come around:" Five cents for a large paper cup, three cents for a small." We did pretty well but usually fought over or drank up the profits.

Like many neighborhoods we had our own bully: Jack Fassett, who liked to pick on my brother and me and all the other kids in the neighborhood. Since being small, having bad eyes, wearing glasses and being heard practicing the piano, I was Jack's perfect target but, since little kids like me have to learn to fight, Jack Fassett picked on me once too often and "Wham, bam! I hit him right smack on his nose. The kids and I "*na na na'd*" him as we watched him running and bawling home to his "mommy" who probably thought he was a bully too. So that was the end of that!

There was this kind of "Tarzanish" jungle called "Dillon's Hollow" down at the end of Fifth Street and one day, I'm climbing around its "cliffs" with some kids, showing off and going from cowboy to Tarzan. I reached out to grab a rock for support and "ouch!" It must not have liked my company because it bit me on my upper leg. Someone rescued me and it was off to the doctor. There I go again! Since then, if the subject of snakes ever comes up, I tell that incident as a reason for not wanting anything to do with snakes. Years later, when my Arizonian friend Mike Karash's dad Joe came to visit, he always brought his homemade cherry wine. *Verrrrry potent*! One day, after slugging down way too much, I told him my snake story. Later, whenever I was with him and others, he'd tell them about the time I said "I was ritten by a battlesnake!"

I've been told I was "bratty" in those days and must have been. Several times my mother tied me to a tree and other times locked me in a closet. Often my father hauled me down to the basement and spanked my butt with a board. Once when my dad was away, my mother tried to spank Bobby and me because we were naughty. All she could muster up was just a soft little pitter-patter" on our soft little asses. So as not to hurt her feelings we both tried hard to work up a cry. We couldn't because the three of us were breaking up laughing. Oh there's more!

One day this kid, Jackie Hower and I decided to skip school and sit on the high bank, up by the college overlooking the Bloomsburg Hospital. The perfect place for throwing stones down at passing cars and we did and we also really caught hell. Then there was the time I was caught playing "doctor" with Freda Polk out in Dillon's Hollow (you show me yours and I'll show you mine) and in fifth grade sometimes I'd be blabbing so much that my teacher made me pull my desk up against hers at the front of the room. When my mother asked why I told her it was because I was "teacher's pet."

This happened in the fourth grade and my English teacher was Miss McKinstry. Miss McKinstry was a tall, husky woman with very short black hair and piercing blue eyes. Most of the time she wore male-like clothes including a tie. However her persona was rather strange because she spoke with a lovely soft voice. I heard that she'd once lifted a naughty kid up in the air by the scruff of his neck.

One day Miss McKinstry named several different books we could choose to read... one being a famous book by Dickens. After giving us some time to think she asked us, one by one, for our choice. When my turn came I stood up and bravely said, "A Sale of Two Titties." Silence... then lots of giggles. Slowly redness began to creep into her face and I thought surely now it was going to be my neck. Suddenly she broke out laughing and the room and I heaved a sigh of relief. Miss McKinstry became one of my all-time favorite teachers. Some kids said she was a "Dyke" but at the time I didn't know what that meant. I could go on and on about being a brat. *My wife still thinks I am!*

Although our town was named Bloomsburg, later it should have been changed to "Mageesburg." That's because Harry L. Magee was the richest, most aggressive and controversial man in town and at the time one of the richest men in Pennsylvania. Although I can't remember ever meeting him, he was a mysterious character and hovered over Bloomsburg like a phantom in the sky.

Harry Laurence Magee, at one time, owned just about everything and everyone in Bloomsburg: the Magee Hotel, the Magee Airport, the Magee Garage, the Magee Museum, and later, the Magee Radio Station. You name it! But most of all, he owned the Magee Carpet Company which rose several red brick stories high and occupied block after block near the Bloomsburg Fair grounds. It was somewhat down the street from where we later lived on West Main Street. At one time or another I'll bet just about everyone of age in Bloomsburg, except my mother and dad, were employed by the huge Magee Carpet Company.

Harry L. was into everything that made money and hated any kind of competition. The day my dad opened a telephone and radio answering service; soon there was a sign on top of a building at the corner of Market and Main streets with the big letters "WHLM," a brand new radio station. Of course everyone knew what that stood for and it's still there. In Pennsylvania, at that time, liquor could only be bought in "State Stores," a real monopoly, and I'm certain it was more than a coincidence that liquor store was in the WHLM building paying a sweet rent to rich old Harry. The more successful my dad was in business Harry L. was right there with his check book out doing the "one up dance." They sure did squabble! Much of the time when I heard my dad mumbling, "God damn, Jesus Christ!" ten to one it had something to do with Harry L. Magee.

A.F. my dad was handsome and always reminded me of Clark Gable without hair. Raised in West Virginia and Maryland, he was uneducated, never having finished school. During his life he only wrote me one letter and I could hardly read it. My "daddy" would never say something like, "I think I'll go." but would say, "I reckon I'll go." He always wore a dark mustache, had beautiful brown eyes, dark whiskers, (before he shaved), and lots of dark hair on his arms which I called "feathers," but not much hair on his head. About 5'8,' he wasn't as tall as I always thought he was when I was a little kid and he never seemed to gain weight. He had the deepest, most beautiful speaking voice you'd ever want to hear, played the uke, and loved to sing: "I'm a Ding Dong Daddy from Dumas" and "When Day Is Done." One day, to my surprise, he opened up my cornet case, took it out and played a tune.

There were a couple things I remember my dad especially liked to do: Almost every Sunday he'd make the most wonderful vanilla ice cream, cranking it up in a shiny silver cylinder in the basement. Hardly an evening went by without his dish of ice cream or bowl of cereal before bed. He loved to go fishing. He'd load our green canoe on top of the car to and away we'd go. I'd watch him, with his long rubber waders on, standing in water up to his hips, casting his fishing pole. Besides, emotional tantrums about Bobby and me and Harry Magee, the only other time I ever saw my dad terribly upset was when Freddie Gould, who worked for my dad, was killed. Freddie was a nice looking, clean-cut, happy go lucky young man who had just gotten married. (Our "darling niece's" husband John Hennessey sure reminds me of Fred.) One afternoon my dad sent Fred out in one of the old station wagons (with the wood on the side) on a job. On a back country road he was struck by another car in an accident that totaled the station wagon and killed Freddie. My father, feeling it should have been him, felt guilty, terribly shaken and depressed. I remember the terrible sight of him crying and striking his head back and forth on a dresser in his bedroom as if to make it all go away. I don't think he ever fully recovered from that.

As stated before, there was always
something going on between my dad and Harry
Magee, but people said A.F. was the only man in
town who ever stood up to Harry L. Magee! The
Magee mansion, several blocks west from where
we lived on West Main Street, was a spacious,
fancy white house, three stories high, with an
indoor swimming pool. After a number of years
Harry would have his house completely torn down
and hauled away, leaving only the pool and a big
empty space. Then right away he'd fill up the
space with a brand new mansion.

Although extremely wealthy, Harry was a
rather pathetic man. According to the story,
during a big forth of July celebration, he ran into a
tree trying to escape from some runaway
fireworks. He was crippled and confined to a
wheel chair for the rest of his life. Harry died in
1972 but his last house remains, having been
donated to the local college by the Magee
Foundation in 1988.

Besides Harry's collection of antiques,
memorabilia, and even railroad and trolley cars,

his biggest prizes were his son Jimmy and his pretty, but chubby daughter Joanne who had a crush on my brother Bob. Although Bob chased after most every other girl in town, he had no eyes to chase after Joanne. *A dumb mistake!* Instead it was Myles Katerman who got Joanne, and along with Harry's son Jimmy, also got the Carpet Mill, everything thing else and some millions of dollars. *Dumb!*

Although my brother Bob comes and goes at various places in these writings... as in my life, I will include here some facts, situations and feelings about him and his part of my life.

My brother Bob (Robert) <u>was</u> dumb and odd in many ways, becoming more so as the years flew by. He was blessed with brains he either never used or misused, but like my dad, was a natural at fixing radios and all kinds of electric stuff at the drop of a hat. Bob was also quite musical playing a smooth violin, a jazzy clarinet or saxophone. One year he almost won the state contest for high school clarinetists. He was three years older than me, taller and rather good looking with blue eyes, brown hair and a dancer's athletic body and was a hell of a good dancer. However, besides having skin that always looked pale, he had terrible taste in clothes and a short temper, which he usually took out on me.

Before we moved to West Main Street, on East Fifth Street we shared a bedroom. I was quite a meticulous little kid and wanted everything right in its proper place. As soon as I'd straighten up the top of our dresser nice and neat and he'd take one look and... *bam...* knock everything off and on the floor. He couldn't wait to pick on me. Once I said something he didn't like and *wham* with his fist in my mouth. I ran up the street to our dentist holding a loose tooth in my mouth with a finger. I put an end to all that one-day when I was home on furlough from military academy. He threatened me and I whopped him and knocked him clear across the bed. He never again laid a hand on me after that but still couldn't resist picking on me or putting me down. My wife, Mary, has always given me hell for that.

22

One person who had Bobby's number was my dad's mother, a chiropractor from Oakland, Maryland. Although a tiny little woman about five feet tall we called her "Big Mamma." If Bob did something she didn't like, when she came to visit, she'd tell my dad and down in the basement he'd go with my dad and a board on his behind. Since she was a Chiropractor, scattered among little glass tubes, her suitcase was always full of garlic. *Whewww, the smell!* but she made the greatest corn bread!

Bob and his wife Velma had five children, my nieces and nephews: Donna Jean, Robert, LuAnna, Kevin and Greg and Penney, a step-child. As he grew older, Bob never changed and sadly, got along badly with some of his kids. He was at times belligerent, nasty, argumentative (even more than me) and a general pain in the ass. He had problems when in the Army, various jobs and during much of his life. He never seemed to finish things he started: model automobiles, renovating rooms, house painting, drawings, divorces, but most importantly college, even a swimming pool.

23

Once, when I came to visit when he was living in Danville, Pa., next to his small house was a great big hole he'd dug. "I'm digging it to make a swimming pool," he said. The next time I visited there was neither a swimming pool nor a hole. He had changed his mind and shoveled all the dirt back.

He was a strange man and it's painful to think about his many problems. And it would be painful for me to go into all of them here. But in his late years he did come to be admired because of his involvement with and dedication to nursing homes and retirement centers in and around Harrisburg. There were those of us who loved him but his strange ways continued when he was ill… right up to his final trip to the hospital. When the ambulance came to pick him up, there he was waiting, sitting on his front stoop because he didn't want anyone to come inside and see the chaotic mess in the house that was indescribable. I was told, after he died in July, 2005, that no one else had been in his house for ten years. He died stubborn, bearded, big bellied, wearing a weird
24

curly hair piece. The truth is I probably loved him but didn't like him. Sad...maybe because I was told a car struck him when he was a little kid up at the intersections of Millville Road, East Street and Main. It is painful to remember him with such negativity as I have discussed many times with Kevin one of his sons. There were many who loved him. There are endless memories related to my brother and this one is a final oddity I thought I'd include:

For Bob's memorial service, I flew from Grand Rapids to Harrisburg for a few days. My plan for returning home was to fly to Lansing, Michigan, change planes and fly home. It was a "dark and stormy day and night" and a long wait at the airport for the flight. Finally, when we took off, it was in the rather late in the evening when we arrived in Lansing. It turned out to be the last arrival of the day and as I embarked every one was scurrying out. Suddenly I realized I was alone on the second floor and in the entire terminal. I proceeded to knock on doors shouting for someone. "Help, some let me outta here! Even the doors were locked to the escalators. I was completely LOCKED IN at the Lansing air terminal.. Luckily I had our cell phone with me but couldn't reach home so I called Kathy, our daughter who was a police woman in California. Kathy is a "if it has to be done, no matter how difficult, she'll find a way to do it" kind of person. A half hour or so latter a policeman appeared at a door. "Your daughter called from California and I'm here to let you out. A cab she ordered is waiting to take you to a motel for the night." My wife Mary drove over and picked me up the next day.

I pause here to say how memories, vague and not so vague, flit in an out of your brain. And sometimes I'm not sure if it's memory or imagination filling in the gaps. And one memory often reminds me of another. I think you might say all along, I've been having "episodic memories" or a sort of "mental time travel."

However my memories of our Christmases in Bloomsburg are quite clear because it was always a big thing. My family, during hard times, was careful about spending money throughout the year except at Christmas time. There were always lots of presents under the tree especially one year.... my favorite of all presents...a chemical set! A cabinet of various bottles of chemicals came attached to a small working table held up by four small legs. I got right at it and proceeded to make my own soap and other things although. my folks were afraid I might concoct something that'd blow up the house. Luckily that was not described in the little book I still have that came with it. *There probably were a few times I would have liked to but never came close to blowing up the house.* My dad was some kind of genius when it came to electrical things and one year he built a circular platform that held our Christmas tree in the middle. A motor was attached to the platform so the tree slowly revolved in a circle. It was circling at Christmas time with a Lionel Electric Train running around the outside for several years.

During those days how could I forget the radio programs? We hovered by our Sparton radio and tuned into the Jack Benny and Fred

Allen shows, listened to the junk falling out of
"Fibber Magee and Molly's closet," the put downs
of Edger Bergman by Charlie McCarthy, and
"Mortimer Snerd" and the spooky "Inter Sanctum"
or *"heh heh heh... the Shadow knows!"* ... even
the gongs of Major Bowes "Amateur Hour."
Whew, so long ago!

For many years the only movie theater in
Bloomsburg was the Capital Theater on Main
Street. There as such a thrill of anticipation when
a big electric organ rose up and Rosie began to
play after the news, comics, and coming
attractions before the feature film. Since Sunday
movies were taboo in Bloomsburg, the four of us
piled into the car and drive forty-two miles up to
the river to Wilkes Barre. Years later a more
modern theater, "The Columbia Theater" opened.
Both the Capital and Columbia theaters are long
gone following the relentless urge of progress,
and the opening of shopping malls. There was a
time when my father was thinking of buying a
drive-in theater. Thank goodness he didn't!

One of my most vivid memories was that of the huge AC&F fire. (AC&F stood for American Car and Foundry). One night, while still living on East Fifth Street, somehow the Foundry caught fire behind our building and I doubt anyone could ever forget that night. The entire factory which ran for blocks and blocks went up in flames. Someone (including my dad) was on every roof in Bloomsburg all night hosing down their roof to prevent flying sparks from catching fire. Hours and hours the fire burned throughout the night, the next day and the next day. Nothing remained but tons of soot, burned debris and what was left of strange huge iron machines, right out of some alien movie, sitting on massive cement foundations. Some good came out of it though. It gave we kids' a unique place to play, especially all of us who were friends of this kid, Dickey Keller.

Dickey was a perky a kid with a small playhouse in his backyard who lived down the street with his dad. The "Our Gang Comedies" of Bloomsburg. Dickey had the playhouse, so of course he was the leader and most of the kids in

the neighborhood wanted to be his friend. We'd
hide out there loafing around doing stuff like
making wooden BB guns with rubber bands
attached that shot BBs. Why? What else... to
shoot each other. Dickey's playhouse was near
the burned out AC&F, a perfect battle ground for
me to get shot in the tongue by a BB . My tongue
swelled up and stung like blazes and for the
longest time "and I *tlalled thike this.*" My mother
took me to the "boys will be boys" doctor again
and it was "no more playhouse or AC&F yard for
you sonny boy!"

However I wasn't finished with Dickey Keller
yet although he and his dad moved to a second
story apartment up town right above the
Woolworth's Five and Dime Store." One night,
when his father was out, Dickey invited me to
come up and play cards. The goodies for the
evening were cold shrimp but. Dickey pipes up:
"Hey, we gotta have somethin' to drink with this
stuff." Out comes a bottle of Tom Collins' mixture
from the fridge. There we were, playing cards,
eating shrimp and gulping down Tom Collin's

Mixture. I don't think I was ever so sick to my stomach except the time, when I was a little kid, my dad caught me either smoking a cigarette and my mother was away somewhere.

At the time my "Uncle Joe" was visiting and my dad and he plopped me down on a high stool in front of the kitchen sink. They handed me a huge cigar and my dad said: "Put this is in that mouth of yours, we want to see you puffing and don't stop 'till its ashes." I puffed for a few minutes then everything "let go" and "let go" I must have turned red white and blue and a little green. It was even worse than the shrimp fiasco. But it did the job and was the beginning and end of my smoking.

Sometimes my mother could be insensitive to both Bobby and me. Like the time we had moved to the tiny town of Espy about a few miles up the road from Bloomsburg. I was still in grammar school, my dad was in Altoona, Pennsylvania managing the radio department in a Montgomery Ward Store and Bobby was somewhere or other. One night my mother (I

31

never understood why) decided to take me to see "The Bride of Frankenstein." at the Capital Theater and I liked to sit by myself way up front. We came in at the "try to destroy the Monster by fire in the Mill scene." Suddenly the "Monster," still alive, stuck his head up out of the well in front of my eyes for the first time. I let out a shriek and tore back down the aisle of the theater shouting, "Mommy, mommy!" We left! Now comes the "mother not so sensitive part." After we'd been home awhile my mother said "Jackie go out and close the garage doors." Close the garage doors? No way! It was dark and I had just had the fright of my life. "Please don't make me do that," I cried and begged. But she wouldn't listen. There I was with a flashlight, groping around, trying to get the damn garage doors closed before the "Frankenstein monster" got me. Scared? I wet my pants!

In many ways, however, my mother was a wonderful mother, wonderful but always busy and extremely self-involved. For instance years later when I was visiting my parents with my wife

Mary, I showed my mother a large composition of mine that had just been published. While glancing at it for a moment she began to talk about the flowers she'd planted up town at the fountain. She had a cute schnauzer dog named Heiji that she adored, I think much more than me, and once at home I played one of my recent piano compositions on the piano. Her response was: "Look, Heiji liked it!" I'll never forget that and now when I play something for someone and the reaction is kinda "duh" I turn to Mary and say: "look Heji likes it!"

A great deal of the time Mary thinks I'm strange and she knew my brother was strange. She believes we inherited it from my mother because we both think my mother was strange. My mother, Dorothy Jean, had an unusual relationship with her friends and what a grudge she could hold! I would be home for a visit and during a conversation she'd say in a sweet voice, "Mrs. Brinton is such a dear friend. She would do almost anything for me."

"And how is Mrs. Ivy?" I'd ask.

"Mrs. Ivy and I aren't speaking," she'd say with a snide sound in her voice.

Next time home I'd ask, "Mother what have you and Mrs. Brinton been up to?"

"Don't you ever mention that name!," she'd say. Then sweetly again, "Mrs. Ivy and I are going shopping later today. I don't know what I'd do without her." The next time it would be the ol' switcheroo.

At times I didn't know how to converse with my mother. Her extreme bias to "Negras" (she called them) stood out like a sore thumb. If I had something positive to say about African Americans she'd say "You don't know what the hell you're talking about! You never saw them like I did home in Birmingham, Alabama in our back yard....filthy, dumb, lazy and couldn't be trusted!" We had many uncomfortable battles about that subject that never got anywhere or changed her mind.

In spite of our differences she and my dad worked their tail off for my brother and me, helped put us through school, sometimes when they couldn't afford it, gave us just about anything we wanted or needed. Although I can't remember my mother ever telling me she loved me but since actions speak louder than words, I'm sure she did.

Like lots of kids, some things we learned on our own, like about sex. I never heard my mother and father discuss that subject and any knowledge about sex came from other kids which especially made me think that sex was naughty. Take the old fashioned word "stripper." I'd heard that word whispered in school, didn't know what it meant but had the feeling it had something to do with girls....probably bad ones.

So one bright sunny day I found myself humming a happy tune and walking down the rail of a railroad track somewhere with a couple of guys. This kid picks up a squiggly little bug off the ground and looks at me with this dumb grin on his face. "It's a stripper," he says. "You gotta sit it

35

on the end of your dick when you're doing stuff
with a girl so's it'll eat all the germs and keep you
from giving her a baby or getting the clap." For
years I was a believer until someone told me (at
least in Bloomsburg) that a "stripper" was another
name for a condom, also called a "rubber." I later
learned that it was really what they called bad
girls who got paid to "show off their boobs and
stuff." I thought that was fun to see because
when I was in my preteens sometimes Vivian
Krickbaum came to our apartment to clean and
also be some sort of a Nanny. She was a young,
lovely buxom woman and she and I both enjoyed
her bathing me in the tub. Especially when she
leaned way over me with all the upper buttons of
her dress unbuttoned. It was probably my first
realization as to the wonderful differences
between girls and boys.

While I'm on the subject of young sex…. on
the other side of the hose house was a lawn
where we played all kind of games like "Red
Rover" and "Hide and Seek." Neither was my
favorite! Behind the firehouse was one of those

basements where you lift up the two doors, close to the ground and go down a few steps into pitch darkness. Myrtle Johnson, the cute, rather "fast" girl next door and a couple of us kids would play "Spin the Bottle." If Myrtle called my name, instead of kissing, we'd lift open the basement doors, hold hands, and go down into the dark. While giggling we'd lower our pants and play "doctor" touching each other "down there."

There were only had a couple girls in our school who were considered "bad." I knew for a fact that Jane Horowitz was because, one day when she saw me alone at school, in the boy's room, she sneaked in and sheepishly asked if she could "watch me pee." I don't remember if I let her or not but probably did.

One day I was searching for something or other and found some "educational" sex books in my parent's dresser. When I read some things my brother told me "daddy and mother did," I was hurt, disappointed and began to cry. I hardly talked to either parent for a week until my brother said it wasn't bad stuff. Then there was "Tondelao!"

Probably Bloomsburg's biggest claim to fame was (and still is) its huge State Fair held every year last week of September. It's probably the largest fair in Pennsylvania..... a magic place for ice cream, hot dog and hamburger stands, a large grandstand to watch acrobats, high wire acts, "The Great Zaccini" shot out of a cannon, sulky harness races, dirt track auto races on Saturdays. Then there were the large long rectangular buildings for farm shows where people stood around looking at and judging cows and pigs and where judges gave out prizes for livestock that were either the biggest or smelled the worst. There were Ferris wheels and thrill rides and what I liked the most, the midway's "James Strates Shows." It was all there at the Bloomsburg Fair. And there was Tondelao!

The fairgrounds were within a short walk when we moved from Fifth Street to West Main Street and at the end of every September the population of Bloomsburg would about triple with

all the "Carnies" and other folks co
fair. It was probably the only tirr
town ever bothered to lock his door. vv.
had his taxi company, "K Kab", he really cleaneu
up at fair time. The "James Strates Shows" which
included sideshows, cupie-doll throwing games,
you name it, was there on the Midway. And
when I was in my early teens the star of the
Strates show was... "Tondelao"!

It was Fair time this day and Jackie Koch,
my best friend and I went down to the fair and
headed for the Midway walking around taking
everything in. Then we heard a guy shouting
"Ton-delay-ooh." There he was, a greasy looking
"barker" standing in front of a small tent shouting
"Tondelao" to a group of people, mostly guys,
gathered around. "You've never seen anything
like her folks! Step up and see Tandelayooooo!"
And hootchy kootching around up on a little
stage, was this tanned, curvy, foreign looking
lady, with long black hair and eyelashes, and
boobs trying to pop out of a skimpy native outfit.
My eyes bugged out of my head. Jackie looked at

39

and I looked at him and surer than the devil
we were going to get into that show. Things were
a lot different in those days, we were kids but
they needed the money and let us in for seventy-
five cents each. Inside was an old scratchy
record player blasting out some funny music and
some guy beating on an old drum. Soon in dances
Tondelao, jumping around shaking her behind and
everything else to the music for about ten
minutes. There were guys with poppin' eyes all
around and Tondelao was smiling and winking at
Jackie and me. When the show was over we
headed out of the tent along with everyone else.
We were at the end of the line, trying to relish
every moment when the barker grabbed us. "Hey
kids," he whispered, "Wanna see the bare ass
parade? It'll only cost ya another quarter." We
weren't sure what he was gabbing about, but the
word "bare" got us and we itched to find out. We
each gave him a quarter and followed him into
another part of the tent. Out came Tondelao with
a smile from here to there. She blinked her eyes,
stopped and stood in front of us backwards. Her
40

bottom wiggled back and forth as down came the back of her jungle outfit until we could see her bare rear, crack and all. Then she starred us in the eye, wet her lips and turned toward us and slowly... ooooh so slowly...pulled the front down. She pulled it down just far enough for us to see a bunch of the thickest blackest, curliest hair I ever saw. Afterwards I thought about Tondelao!. I dreamed about Tondelao! I can almost see her now and I've never passed the big fair grounds in Bloomsburg again without thinking about Tondelao.

Music! It seems like music has occupied most of my life. The story goes that when I was just four years old with my mother at her good friend the Feldman's house, I heard some music on the radio and went to their piano and plunked out some of the notes. Mrs. Feldman, a very good pianist, was so impressed that she suggested my parents buy a piano. I wasn't much older when I played in my first piano recital at the Capital Theater. Barely reaching the keys, I was lifted onto the piano bench. When the story's told it seems to impress anyone since they probably think I was playing Mozart or Bach. Unfortunately I have to explain that it was only a little piece called "Frisky Lambs" but they still think it was pretty damn early.

Once, when I was very small and with my mother in New York City, she took me to the top of the Empire State Building where a giant of a man, with a strange accent, lifted me up by the seat of my pants. He carried me around the dome so I could look out and see the entire magnificent city. When we visited New York I couldn't wait to open the glass compartments of the Horn and Hardart Automat to grab a sandwich or large piece of pie. They were finally done in by McDonalds and other fast food restaurants and I've always missed them.

My mother was conscientious about Bobby and my having music lessons because she drove through pouring rain and snow to take us to our violin and cornet lessons at Susquehanna University. At the time I was also taking piano lessons with Miss Christian in Bloomsburg. Miss

Christian was a average pleasant teacher, not very strict, and I always looked forward to my lessons. One day she invited Jeannie Knight and me to her farm and told us we were her favorite pupils. It was especially lots of fun because Jeannie and I played Tarzan and Jane in the barn haytstacks.

I always thought any musical talent I'd inherited was from my mother. I'll tell you the real story later. My mother (Dorothy Jean, aka D.J.) was a dancer and at a young age and in her early teens joined the "Zeigfield Follies." She was a southern gal from Alabama and a wonderful tap and toe dancer. Blond, lovely, petite with blue eyes, she had strong perfect dancer legs and a stronger will and disposition. Early in her teens, after the "Follies," she was on the road, traveling around the country doing shows with Eddie Cantor. I have a wonderful picture of Eddie with the inscription: "To Dorothy who is as cute as can be, Love, Eddie Cantor." Much later she opened a dance studio in Bloomsburg and I'll bet there wasn't a family in town, sometime or other;

whose kid didn't take a dancing lesson from my mother. And that included my brother and me. Hardly a week went by when we weren't tap dancing somewhere for someone.

Each year one of the biggest events in town, along with graduation and May Day, was Dorothy Jean's dance recital, held in the Bloomsburg High School auditorium. D.J. was remarkable since she created the theme and choreography for a ballet, designed the costumes and lighting, helped make the scenery and solicited the advertisements for the program she prepared. Standing in the wings, with a beautiful corsage pinned to her brand new gown, she'd be "One, two, step, hop" rhythmically to all the little kids if they forgot their dance steps. I was self-conscious and not a very good dancer, but my brother Bobby was terrific. He always got the best parts in the section of the recital I hated the most.... the Ballet! He was alays the "Prince" or something splendid while I was always some silly thing like a chicken or "the cock crowing in the morning," Once, during a show in Catawissa, I
44

was dancing an "Apache" number with Gerry Fegley. The Apache dance was supposed to be rough and tough like George Raft in Paris. I was being rough and got so carried away that I threw poor Gerry into the footlights. There was this great big "pop and crack" of broken lights so loud I thought everyone would head for the exits. You might say: I stopped the show!

I was a pretty good singer though, especially when I was either down on one knee singing "Mammy" like Al Jolson, or singing love duets with Gloria Yurkovsky. Gloria's mother was the typical showbiz pain in the butt" mother but Gloria was shapely, beautiful and my mother's best ballet student. She was sort of the "Prima Ballerina" of Columbia County. Naturally I had a crush on her but I believe most of my affection was because several times she loaned me her bicycle.

One May Day, while in grammar school and how it ever happened, I was voted Prince Charming with Jeannie Knight as Cinderella. Big deal! Our prize was dancing around the may pole together, which wasn't so great because it made me dizzy. Besides Jeannie Knight I had crushes on girls way back in the second grade and wrote notes like "Mary Lou, I love you" to the brightest girl all through school, Mary Lou Fenstemacher. But my first big love was Patricia Hemingway.

I first met Pat when we were in our early teens in high school. Since her mother and father were recently divorced it was summers with father in Bloomsburg, and the rest with mother in Charleston, West Virginia. I saw Pat for the first time from our window. There she came, devilish pretty, slim and blue-eyed with bright red lipstick, walking up the street in tight short shorts, swinging her slender girlish hips and strutting a big white and black spotted Dalmatian on a long leash. She was a definite "no no" in Bloomsburg. Obviously used to being stared at, she'd keep on walkin' and a shakin' her cute little fanny, smiling, looking straight ahead like she didn't give a damn....and she didn't! I can still see that special cunning expression on her face. Her lips would curl up at the ends and her dimpled half smile

46

would make you think she was about to do something naughty, which she usually did...or wanted to do. Every kid in town thought she was the "cat's meow" and, of course, parents didn't approve of her... including mine. (My Mother, whenever she didn't like the way someone looked or acted, squinted up her nose and said: "We don't go for that in Bloomsburg!) That was another good reason for me to be totally smitten and determined to become Patty's best beau.

One evening when she was sitting alone, sucking on a coke in Moyer Brothers drug store, I got up enough nerve to strike up a conversation. Probably because she liked music and maybe heard me play the piano she let me walk her all the way home. We sat and talked, swinging on her porch swing just like the in movies, Just at the right moment (also like the movies) I decided the best way to impress her was to sing. So I did my "Nelson Eddy" bit and sang: "The Breeze and I." Thus now the moment for the big kiss! "Wop!" she gave me a hell of a slap on the face. That never happened to Nelson! It sure broke the spell in a hurry. It must have had some effect because soon we started "going steady." At night I'd sneak out to see her every chance I had. I'd crawl out on a little balcony from our bedroom on the second floor, climb down, and scurry to the other end of town.

Pat Hemingway was one sly chick and had lots of tricks. Besides stealing apples from people's trees she had a trick I'll never forget. Every year in our neighborhood the fire company, next door, held a small street carnival. East Fifth Street was blocked off and filled with a number of small booths, some games, and some food. One of the booths had a Los Vegas like spinning wheel that drew Pat to it like a mouse to cheese when I once took her to the carnival. We were the only ones at the booth and Pat went into action. You put coins on a number you hoped matched where the wheel stopped and the man spun the wheel. Pat would smile at the guy working the wheel and place coins on her number, keeping her hand close, as the wheel spun. Then as the wheel slowed to a stop she'd give the guy on the wheel the eye and a wide-dimpled smile, engaging him in conversation. She'd quickly glance at the wheel then slyly move her coins over to the winning number as the guy, entranced, smiled back. Once she did this three times in a row and got a way with it. Look folks! We have a winner here!

I thought the best thing to come from our move from East Fifth Street to West Main Street was that it brought me up a couple blocks from Pat Hemingway but I was suddenly broken hearted when she suddenly had to return back to West Virginia. After she left I was in a movie at the Capital Theater and there was a cute, light haired little girl named Marian Schlaw sitting in front of me. She and another girl were giggling and the girl turned and whispered, "Did you know Marian likes you?" I didn't but I did then and she came back and sat next to me. It was the beginning of another little fling but my heart was really back in Charleston with Patty Hemingway. When something changed in Pat's family and she suddenly came back to Bloomsburg, I dropped Marian like a hot potato and feeling guilty, whenever I saw Marian again, I'd cross to the other side of the street. What a rat!

As happens most of the time, with childhood puppy love, when I left Bloomsburg, Pat and I lost track of one another. Years later, while in the army at Fort Dix, New Jersey, I ran across her in New Hope, Pennsylvania, kind of an arty little town. She'd been married once unsuccessfully and was there running a little boutique shop with another woman who I suspected was Pat's lover. I wasn't too surprised because I knew she would try anything that might make her happy. Sadly, a few years later, I heard that Pat had died from an over dose of drugs. One of our book club books was about a very lovely rather rebellious girl named "Daisie Miller" by Henry James. I hardly read a page without being reminded of Patty Hemingway.

When I was a kid I was confused about so many family things. I'd seen pictures of me as a baby carried by my mother in "The Garden Of the Gods" in Colorado. I'd seen other pictures of me being held by people I didn't know or never saw

before. My brother had a violin and a violir
that looked like a round black cannon. Where did
that come from? I remember once a cute little
girl, Shelley, who reminded me of Shirley Temple,
came to visit us for a while. No one ever
explained her, who she was or to whom did she
belong except I was told she was a cousin. How
did I come to be born in Colorado Springs
Colorado when we were all from the East or
South? Who was the strange little man in the
funny hat, in the very old picture standing next to
someone who looked like my mother? One day
Velma, my brother's wife, told my first wife Nancy
the story then Nancy told me this story:

One year, in the twenties, a very young
Jewish musician, Irving Rosasarakoff (I never saw
the correct spelling of his name) came to this
country from Russia by way of Ellis Island. There
were no details as to why he came, but probably
because back in the 20's, as depicted in the
musical "Fiddler On the Roof," Jews, as they
always seem to be, were being persecuted in
Russia. Irving was an excellent young violinist

and conductor, thus the strange violin   now belonging to my brother. Irving (also my brother's middle name) must have been a fine musician because he was with the Zeigfield Follies where he met my mother the dancer. He had either changed his name to Rosen, or it was changed for him. My mother and Irving married and joined a traveling show starring Eddie Cantor. Irving Rosen was my biological father and Andrew Filson Kimmell was my stepfather who, I assume, adopted Bob and me. Although I was completely surprised I have never been upset about it because all those things I had wondered about began to make sense. Years later after my stepfather (in 1985) and mother, (in 1988) were gone, my wife Mary and I came upon newspaper articles about Irving. My real father had contracted tuberculosis, as he was about to conduct an orchestra in Colorado and died in a sanitarium at the foot of Pikes Peak shortly after I was born.   Never ever did my stepfather, brother or mother discuss any of this with me.

I've thought many times how this all came about and came to this possible conclusion: I believe there were some negative relations between my real father's Jewish family and my stepfather. A.F. or Fil as he was called was very prejudiced, especially about Irving's family who probably wanted to be involved with their grandchildren. Fil never hesitated to remind us of his dislike for: "Jews (Kikes), Polacks, Niggers, Waps or Spics." On the wall, in our bedroom, in Grand Rapids, Michigan, is a picture, of my stepfather and my mother. Next to it is a picture of my mother and a small man with a somewhat pronounced nose, wearing a funny hat and very foreign looking bow tie and suit... Irving Rosasarakov, my father. Now anyone who knows the story mentions "my musical genes." because of my biological father

My High School days were days during the time of the big swing band....Tommy and Jimmy Dorsey, Benny Goodman, Artie Shaw, Harry James and all those other great bands. There were also bands we called "Mickey Mouse Bands:"

Sammy Kaye, Guy Lombardo, Blue Barron and Tommy Tucker, ricky-ticky bands that played gushy dance music played for old folks. Rock stars today, bands and their vocalists stars of yesterdays like the Eberly brothers, Ella Fitzgerald, Helen O'Connell, Jo Stafford, "The Pied Pipers," "Modernairs," and Tommy Dorsey's Frank Sinatra. I saw many of them at the Strand, Capital and Paramount Theaters in New York before or after a movie.

Most of the kids, during that time, were jitterbugging after school. I always wondered how they could look right at each other and do all that stuff without being embarrassed...arms and legs flinging, panting, sweating, staring at each other with "I know it all" "ain't we the birds" look on their faces, smiling ear to ear. I still don't understand when I see them today! While they were jumping and flailing around like clowns, I'd be down the street at the house of two fine musician friends, Dayton and Jim Greenly listening to Glenn Miller records, and trying to copy down the arrangements.

Although I was thought to be talented in music, I was never a particularly good student in school...I doubt not because of lack of brains. Probably boredom, laziness or total involvement with music. Also I never went to Kindergarten and skipped a grade in grammar school. For more excuses I might add: being extremely self-conscious because of being younger than most, several inches shorter than everyone in my class, practically blind in one eye, and wearing glasses since my face was big enough to hold them. A saving grace: I did love to read!

Rafael Sabatini books, "Captain Blood" and "Scaramouche" and books by Charles Dickens and Dumas were all favorites. But did I ever enjoy the adventures of Buck Rogers, Dick Tracy and others in "Big Little Books!" What I liked the best were pulp magazines especially "Doc Savage." Once a month I saved some money, walked across East Street to Carter's store and bought the latest issue. I couldn't wait to read the next exciting story about "the Man of Bronze," and his assistants, the chemist Monk, Ham his lawyer and the others.

In Junior and Senior High School I played piano in the orchestra and first trumpet in the concert and marching bands. I listened to lots of records and studied a bunch of jazz piano books like Art Tatum, Jelly Roll Martin, Alec Templeton, Mary Lou Williams and Teddy Wilson. Although I was classically trained, I learned to play chords necessary to be a swing band or jazz piano player. Sometimes I played for my mother's dance classes and I'm certain it helped me become a fast reader. I was especially good on the eighty-eights playing boogie-woogie. At my high school graduation, I was asked to play the piano and while climbing up several stairs to the stage to play a boogie-woogie solo, my large, ill-fitting graduation gown caught under me and little Jackie Kimmell, stumbled and almost fell. But I made it, sat down, and wailed out eight to the bar!

One summer, my brother and I and the Feldman brothers received scholarships to "The

Ernest Williams Summer Music Camp" in the Catskill Mountains. It was quite a contribution to our musical education. One of my lasting memories was about a tall, skinny kid, Robert Craft, who was a hell of a trumpet player. One day, while diving in the swimming pool, he hit his head on the edge of the diving board and had to leave camp. Several years later, when I was a cadet at New York Military Academy, I heard about a "Robert Craft" who had just graduated the year before and had a great reputation as a trumpet player. Years later, when reading an article about Igor Stravinsky, I noticed it was written by Robert Craft. Curious to learn more, I learned that he not only wrote articles and books about Stravinsky, but also championed him, conducted his music, and lived with Stravinsky and his wife when the composer became an American citizen living in California. Looks like he recovered pretty well from his head injury! The only other things I recall about the Ernest Williams Camp was my playing the piano for the opera "Faust" and the food that was so bad that mama came and got the four us out of there!

Religion didn't play an important part of our family life at first but I finally "saw the light" when I started paling around with Jackie Koch my best friend in high school. Jackie was a devout Episcopalian acolyte and introduced me to the Episcopal Church. I was confirmed in the Church, did the training thing learning all the necessary creeds, and became a full-fledged Acolyte. On Fridays, we'd leave high school during the day, put on a long bright red cassock, and an innocent face, go down the street to the church and serve bread and wine for communion as Priest Servers. It was, at that time, all morally satisfying, however one day I came to the realization that my sudden interest in religion might have been for a more important reason...our meeting girls at Episcopal Church conventions.

Jackie Koch was quite a blond haired handsome kid. He led rather a unique life because his dad was the dean of men up at the college. Jack and his family lived in a small apartment in the men's dorm. Being around college guys most of the time, Jack was always "wise cracking," always with a smart and witty come back. When I broke my ankle playing football and we'd be walking down the street, Jack would run out in front of me, turn around, make like he had a fishing rod and shout, "reeling in the fish!" When we passed someone, he'd ask him or her to sign my cast which became overflowing with names. A hit with the girls he was also the best ping-pong and tennis player I ever knew. One day he and his family moved away and sadly to say, he was another very close friend I never saw again.

My dad was a self-made man with the perfect partner in my mother who was a real go-getter, and non-stop woman. The two of them were addicted to work and were always on the go deciding what next to do next to make money. In the beginning, at least when we first lived in Bloomsburg, we sold and repaired Spartan radios and refrigerators in our little store on Fifth Street. After a number of years, we opened a children's apparel store called "Kimmell's Kiddy Shop" in

Berwick, twelve miles up the highway which didn't work out too well so they opened the same store back in Bloomsburg.   Not too great either so they closed the store or A.F. took a job (as I mentioned earlier) in Altoona.   That lasted about a year and it was not only back to Bloomsburg for us, but strangely enough, back to the same building on East Fifth Street, which must have been waiting for us because it was still vacant..

About that time my dad met Ben Sterling, a wealthy businessman in Scranton. Ben owned a hotel, and amusement park besides jukeboxes and pinball machines all over the mid-eastern part of Pennsylvania. Needing a repairman and associate to keep things working he met my dad and discovered he was perfect for the job. Ben retired soon afterwards and sold the business to my dad. It proofed to be the beginning of better days for the Kimmell family. At times I would go and help change records on he juke boxes and collect coins from the machines, stacking up coins to put in little folders. I was very good at dropping coins on the floor and my dad, not being the most patient person in the world, used a favorite phrase which he often applied: "Can't you <u>ever</u> do anything right?" (After hearing one of my early compositions, he said: "Why the hell don't you write a ***!!! polka instead and make us some money?") He must have been referring to the record, "Pistol Packin' Momma." That got so many plays that often the needle went practically all the way through the record. My mother often said the take from that record paid for a year of my future college.

We finally began to make a lucrative living so we bought a rather large apartment building on West Main Street. My mother's office, dance studio and dad's repair shop were on the basement floor; our apartment on the second and on the third floor was several other apartments we rented out. A gas station, which we bought, was also on the front corner of the building. One summer I put on a cap, scrubbed people's windshields, checked their oil and sold gas for about forty-five cents a gallon. We didn't have to go far to buy the gas because there was a railroad track right next to our building that supplied our large backyard tanks with gasoline. I remember how the house shook when the train came by.

As long as we had to buy records for the jukeboxes we decided to sell the gas station and open up a record store in the building, where I also worked from time to time. When the local taxi company was up for sale, my dad bought that too and called it "K Cabs." At the same time he was making a bundle installing all the new refrigeration in the Geisinger Memorial Hospital in Danville. (Wow, just like Harry Magee!)

Next there was a spectacular large white house several miles away in Danville, right on the Susquehanna River, which featured an ornate spiral staircase and a long white porch facing the river which afforded a beautiful view. It had recently been remodeled into apartments, had tenants and was for sale. Dad and Mom liked it....they bought it. I was there with my mother a few days helping to plant flowers. She loved it and I hated every minute of it...I still do! They weren't finished buying, because later they closed the record store, opened a radio and telephone answering service where they hired employees, and bought another apartment building in Sunbury about twenty miles away. They didn't seem to enjoy luxury for themselves and it was kind of sad their still living in the apartment there and working and working! And my mother was still teaching dancing lessons and working in the business offices with a few other employees. It was certainly fortunate for my brother and me because after they were gone we were able to reap the rewards.

The Poconos and Those Glorious Days

Without a doubt some of the best times I can remember were the summers I spent in the Pocono Mountains before or after my last year of high school. The times are rather jumbled together, in my mind, and I'm not quite sure which summer something happened or with whom.

The Pocono Mountains are part of the Appalachians, in the eastern part of Pennsylvania, around the town of Stroudsburg and about sixty-five miles from Bloomsburg. Hobie Feldman (one of the brothers from my earlier "Ernest Williams days") asked me, at the end of a school year, if I'd like to be a waiter-musician at a rather small Pocono summer lodge called "The Pleasant Ridge House" in a tiny town called "Mountainhome." There would only be a couple of us so I accepted the job and it would be kind of like a paid vacation. We'd wait on tables during the days and play music in a small rec room for dancing and romancing in the evenings. Any time we weren't working we would be allowed to join in with the guests and do just about anything we wanted to do... or get away with.

I played a big, old upright piano, somewhat out of tune, but considering everything, I didn't much care. The Lodge was a medium large white wooden building with a long front porch that had the most wonderful cold spring water coming out of a shiny brass medal lean-over-to-drink water fountain. There was a shuffleboard court at the end of the porch, a tennis court in front and above on a hill, a moderately sized swimming pool. The lodge opened the Fourth of July and closed on Labor Day and was owned and run by the Jannings family. Old man Jannings was a medium tall, skinny, grouchy old guy who was always scratching around pretending he was the boss. His wife, the general manager, was a shriveled up, bespectacled, high-screeching, cranky old lady who looked like the witch in "the Wizard of Oz! But it was their son Don, a strong, well organized, husky, good looking, hardworking man with a slow-droning voice and his soft-spoken pretty wife, Wanda, who <u>really</u> ran the place.

Most of the visitors on vacation were young ladies and families from the cities of Philadelphia and New York who wanted to get away from it all but couldn't afford anything ritzy. Pleasant Ridge House was THE place to come! The lodge featured home cooked food served in "American Style," which meant large dishes of mashed potatoes, rolls and vegetables served on long tables for all to select. The meat and desert (delicious home-baked pies and ice cream) were ordered and served individually. There was tennis, swimming, beer and wiener roasts at night up on the hill, hayrides, shuffleboard, horseshoes and bowling. All the stuff that folks who weren't highfalutin would like to do. For a little more excitement away from the lodge there were hikes to Rattlesnake Falls, square dancing at Ottawa Lodge, movies at a close by theater at Buck Hill Falls Lodge, and the evening dancing to "the band."

The most pleasant thing about the Pleasant Ridge House was the turn over every week or so of single young women who came to relax from their sometimes-boring jobs and maybe even have a romantic fling. I was young but old in female appreciation. I had two basic appreciations in life....music and girls! Every week the guys and I would stand around watching the new cars arrive, checking out some cute chick saying, like some big macho dude: "that one's mine."

The first summer when Jackie Koch was there, we invented what we called "The Pirates Club." To join we had to drink, bottoms up, a huge glass filled with whiskey, rum, vodka, gin, brandy and scotch all mixed together. It was the only time in my life I ever passed-out stinking drunk. Then there was the so called "Social Director my first summer who's name was Alex.

Alex was a skinny, Russian looking percussionist from Hazleton, Pennsylvania in his mid twenties whose sole purpose in life, besides playing all kinds of drums, was all kind of women and what he thought they were only good for....sex! For example: our bedroom with four or five cots and its own bathroom was about four stairs up and at the further end of the kitchen. And on the other side of our wall was an extra room for guests. Besides, thinking up ways to entertain the guests, one of Alex's duties was to help assigning rooms. One day we saw him punching several small holes through to the other room in our wall. And who would Alex assign to that room? Three lovely young ladies! He reminded us, the innocents that we were, to be up at the pool awaiting the moment the ladies headed to their room to change after a swim. Down the hill we'd run, heading for the bedroom just in time for the peeking "naked ladies show." Later we found that he'd cut holes in the attic of the building, directly above beds. We thought watching a couple maybe on their honeymoon was going too far. His addiction caught up with him because someone squealed and Alex was gone! The next summer there was a new Social Director by the name of Max, and he was another story.

Max was a husky, six-foot, athletic, blue eyed, good looking young guy. A good tennis player with a smooth manner, everyone liked Max. One afternoon, when we were outside with some of the guests, Max suddenly fell over and began thrashing about on the ground moaning and frothing at the mouth. We were all scared and I thought it might be an epileptic seizure. Luckily some guest, who knew more about it, told us to hold Max down so as not to hurt himself. Then he stuck something in the poor guy's mouth to keep him, so he said, from biting his tongue. Max finally stopped thrashing and fell into a deep sleep and in about an hour was awake, embarrassed and taking some kind of medicine. It was the conversation of the day and unfortunately the next day Max was gone.

My favorite employee at Pleasant Ridge House was the cook Anna a black short and stout lady who was the spitting image of Aunt Jamima …especially with that bandana thing wrapped around her head. Anna was a pleasant, delightful, wonderful "meat and potatoes" cook. She had a sharp, witty tongue and must have liked me special. Every day she baked pies for the guests and every few days or so she'd bake an extra pie just for me which I'd sneak up stairs to our bedroom.

The capacity of the lodge was maybe ninety to a hundred people and there were times I might be waiting on forty people. I was a fast little guy who was in one swinging door and out the other, carrying as huge a tray as I could handle. All smiles, as pleasant as could be at Pleasant Ridge House, I played good dance music, worked hard, catered to the guests (especially the young ladies) and was always busy figuring out new ways to get good tips.

I especially remember one family, very English, the Micklebergs who returned often but Papa Mickleburg would come for a day or two then leave. Their daughter, Pat, was a lovely bosomy, kinky-haired young lady who, their first season, switched her attentions back and forth from Jackie Koch to me. Besides my usual duties, my orders were to stop whatever I was doing, around four in the afternoon, take a cup of hot tea from the kitchen, find Mrs. Mickleberg and serve her. Each time, at the end of their stay, I'd have to walk around the grounds searching and picking up her empty cups and saucers.

One day, in the afternoon, when I was in the dining room setting up for dinner, Don Jannings hollered that I had a phone call. I picked up the phone and it was some guy with a story about my playing the piano for Fred Waring. at a famous golf resort "Shawnee on The Delaware. I said "Who's this, and it's not a funny joke" and hung up. The phone rang again and it was really a legitimate deal. They wanted me, they needed me, and it's a good feeling to be needed!

Fred Waring was a famous, popular bandleader and choral director and his orchestra was "Fred Waring and the Pennsylvanians." At the time he probably did more for choral music than anyone else. He was also the owner of this spacious lodge, (Shawnee On the Delaware) not too far from Pleasant Ridge House. Waring had assembled a band to play for the summer but the piano player suddenly was taken ill so they needed someone in a hurry. From the Pocono grapevine, they heard, although I was just a kid, I was a good pop pianist and a fast reader. An outfit would be ready for me and they needed me to play that evening.

An hour or so later a long black limo picked me up and took me to a lovely large sort of Vee shaped lodge in the middle of a huge golf course. On the stage in the dining room, was a white grand piano and a stack of piano music. I looked over some of the arrangements they were going to play, fitted in an outfit and scared as hell at first, played for dancing that evening with some damn good musicians from the "Pennsylvanians." They were pleased! Afterwards I was asked if I could stay for another day.

Fred Waring (who wasn't the warmest person I'd ever met) was a good-looking man with wavy hair and a face that was perfect for the commercial music world. Tom, his brother, was warm and friendly, an interior decorator who had created most of the decor at the lodge. Fred's lovely, exotic looking wife was not only the lodge hostess but also was one of the featured dancers. Maybe the reason for Fred's rather cold demeanor was because of his wife's affair with her dark, handsome dancing partner Drago. I also met a friendly kid, about my age, whose father worked for Waring Enterprises and was the actual inventor of the "Waring Blender." How strange things can be because my first published compositions for chorus were published by Shawnee Press owned by Fred Waring. I recently read, in a book by Ian Carr, that the great jazz pianist, Keith Jarrett, had once had a job working for Fred Waring, and had played the same piano at Shawnee with a Dixieland band.

Maybe I should have advertised myself as the "Sick Man's Relief Pianist" because many years later, living in Scottsdale, Arizona, I received a call in the early morning from the manager of the then Glenn Miller band. They were engaged to perform in Flagstaff at Northern Michigan University and (guess what?) their pianist was suddenly taken ill. Could I come up and play? Wife Mary and I drove up and there I was...on stage playing a concert grand piano with the Miller Orchestra, performing mostly old original Miller arrangements which included the present vocal group "The Modernaires." We were all surprised because the young student body loved it and shouted for more.

I'm having a difficult time trying to remember how the war fit into my life in those times being young and far removed. I do recall the news of Pearl Harbor, the gas sticker on our car and reports one time or another of someone I knew being killed in the service. Also my brother was drafted into the Air Force while I was enjoying the Poconos, where every time an airplane flew overhead late, Betty Angelmire, Wanda's sister would look up in the sky up and say, "Here comes Hitler!"

At Pleasant Ridge House, one of my summers, Betty was hired, along with Esther Smith to be the cleaning up girls, making beds and generally doing necessary chores. Betty, a

74

few years older than me, was a lovely, five foot five, brown eyed, full bosomed, wholesome, naive girl from "down on the farm," who probably had never known a musician before, or at least one who didn't play hoedowns. Our romance started soon after the season began in the evening when I asked her for a Sunday stroll down a narrow little road to the "Log Cabin" a small ice cream and general hangout. It was a half moon, star lit, beautiful night and after some ice cream, we walked, hand-in hand on the way back, stopping on a little bridge, as the song goes "to linger awhile." How lovely the evening was, how lovely Betty was and what a nice guy I am, etc. This, led to soft kisses on her lips on that sweet little bridge. After that it was hay rides together, beer and hot dogs on the hill together, Buck Hill Falls movies together; and romantic evening walks. We were in love! Don Jannings was his usual suspicious self and continually groaned while his wife Wanda was happy for her sister. "He's a nice bright talented young man...a little young, but who knows?" The summer days drifted down and

Betty and I we were an established couple.... the farmer's daughter and the musician.

I had her all to myself for the rest of the summer and maybe...forever... or at least right up until cute little Bunny Grooms from Philadelphia came along. Or was it Delores Lilljenstein from Freehold, New Jersey, or Terry from Scranton or. ...??? And Betty saw and Betty knew and was hurt and Jack was a dumb idiot kid, an insensitive adolescent and it was much too soon to get serious and probably more interested in the female body than the female mind. Sometimes Betty stayed in her room all day and refused to work, which resulted in anger and daggers from Esther Smith and especially Wanda. Since Wanda was in a dither there was holy hell from Don. I was in everybody's doghouse. Things were in a general uproar and I was about to be fired. Soooo...I repented and it was only Betty Anglemire for the rest of the summer.

When the summer was over I visited Betty at her family's farm. Her somewhat gruff father, in his overalls and mother in her print dress and

76

apron, accepted me warmly. They even thought of me, in spite of being so young, as maybe a future husband someday for their precious daughter. I'd help work the farm!

After my last the season at Pleasant Ridge was over, I invited Betty to take a bus and come to Bloomsburg to meet and visit my family. My mother thought she was a "sweet wholesome girl and a good cook" and actually liked her. After her visit Betty and I headed back to her home in the Poconos on a bus. My mother thought we'd be back down on the farm, and Betty's mother thought we'd still be in Bloomsburg. But we were in between in a nice cozy room at the Sterling Hotel in Wilkes Barre, Pa. I have no recollection whatsoever as to how we were able to get that room. I've searched my brain trying to remember how my romance with Betty Angelmire played out but obviously it disappeared like all the others so far. It's almost impossible to imagine that if she were still alive today she might be someone's grandmother or even great grandmother. I believe we'd rather remember someone who had been especially close to us and part of our past, remember them as they were when we last knew them. I think back with sadness on those glorious wonderful care free days with hardly a worry in the world, feeling physically and mentally strong...my days back in the Pocono Mountains.

When I graduated from high school it was decided I was too young (and too immature?) for college. Fortunately, because of my ability playing the cornet (trumpet), I received a music scholarship to the New York Military Academy which was kind of a prep school for West Point. The Academy was (and still is) situated in Cornwall-On-Hudson, New York, right up the Hudson from West Point and about sixty miles north of New York City. For two semesters, I'd be taking a postgraduate course. I never imagined I'd be wearing a flashy West Point-like cadet uniform, saluting every time I turned around and carting around a rifle... but there I was Jack the "Soldier." But I didn't get off to a very good start.

Sometime during the first week, at dinnertime in the large mess hall, we all poured in and sat down at long tables for evening chow. A couple of civilians strolled in, way over at the other side of the mess hall. One of them caught my attention, and my attention must have caught

someone else's attention. I noticed, and must
have starred at a lovely young lady who sat and
down for dinner. I was surprised as she seemed
out of place amongst all the males. When our
chow was over I was told to report to Major
Kuwait, the Commanding Officer. Soon I was
standing at attention before a middle-aged,
shorthaired, clipped-voiced, medal-covered, I
mean business uniformed officer. "God damn it,
Cadet Kimmel," he snarled. "That young lady you
were staring at today is a daughter of one of our
professors here and god damn it she has just as
much right to be here as you do!" (His face was a
little red now) "So you keep your god damn eyes
to yourself and don't let happen again!. Do you
understand Cadet Kimmel? If it does, your ass is
in serious trouble! Now get the hell out!" So
much for my first day!

I was in the Academy band, and when we
weren't marching, we were playing for the Corp or
parts of the Corp so they could" hut two three
four" and "hut two three four" some more.. One
of the members of the band was a little short guy,
80

about five three, wearing thick horned-rimmed glasses and a butch haircut and blowing a trombone. He was appropriately called "Stumpy" Brown and he and I became good friends. Stumpy Brown's brother, Les Brown the famous bandleader had been a cadet earlier. I was surprised later, while reading a biography of Stephen Sondheim, that he too had once been a New York Military cadet. Good company!.

Some years later when in Chicago, while playing with a trio at the Palmer House, I went to the Sheridan Hotel to hear "Les Brown and His Band of Renown." And there he was... little "Stumpy" Brown, sitting in the trombone section with his big bass trombone, wailing away. It was also quite a memorable experience because, on a break, we had a chance to talk and he introduced me to a very young, lovely lady who was the present singer with the band. .Doris Day! Before she became a big star her career had begun with the band. Some other cadets who had attended the Academy were: Robert Craft (who I earlier discussed), Francis Ford Coppola, Troy Donahue,

and the musician and fine arranger Johnny
Mandel. Indeed I was in good company.

Since I was a "New Cadet" I was at the
bottom of the barel. New cadets had to take a lot
of crap and participate in ridiculous, infantile
hazing like eating a "square meal" in the mess
hall and all kind of assorted hazing. I was my
usual feisty self and got into lots of scraps, but I
had become a pretty good boxer and could handle
myself even for a little guy. I was a tough little
son of a bitch and was rooming with another
tough son of a bitch, a big strong "old cadet" who,
when I needed it, protected me. But I fought
most of my own battles...as with the Newman
Twins.

The Newman Twins were fairly tall, slinking,
dark haired, bespectacled, exact look-a-likes "old
cadets." They were always sneaking around,
getting into things where they didn't belong and
generally pissing everyone off including me. They
liked to pick on me with knee bends and pushups
every time they spotted me. One very cold night,
when I was sound asleep in my cot, they threw

snow on me from the roof. Then in my wet pajamas made me go out on the roof and shovel snow in the middle of the night. I got pretty sick with my sinuses and had to be taken to a doctor in Newburgh to get "flushed out." One day, however, I caught them snooping around inside my locker and that was the "lick that killed dick"! With guys standing around on the second floor of the barracks, I tore into them and got both down on the floor. With my arms around one's neck, and my legs around the others, I squeezed and squeezed as hard as I could until they started to cry and moan and say my name. That must have gained me respect with all the guys because when came the day for my graduation from a new cadet to an old, I had to run the "gauntlet".... that is guys on each side of a long line with whipping belts. I thought I might be whipped raw but they let me run all the way through without anyone lifting a belt. I took my turn playing reveille in the morning and taps at night, and if we had to spit, when we stood in formation, we had to shout, "Spec rate sir?" Being at the Academy was one of the few times my father ever came to see or hear me do anything. I have some pictures, dressed in my uniform and he's standing next to me, looking proud as can be... probably one of the few times ever. During my short year at the academy I was a good student and retook some subjects I hadn't done well in high school and aced them all.

We had several intramural football teams and I was on one playing halfback. In those day guys played defense and offense both and I was a pretty good tackler for a small guy. I was also a fast runner and thought I could just about out-run anyone. We were playing a game one afternoon and I was running like lightning with the ball heading for a touchdown. I looked behind me and there was this guy gaining on me by the second like he was shot out of cannon. Wham, down I went! An early lesson learned: everything you think you can do so well, someone else can do better.

The Academy had a great varsity football team, which, at that time, had always been one of the best in the country for a prep school. The band accompanied the football teams for a couple of games, one especially being the big "Little Army-Navy Game" with Admiral Farragut Academy in Pine Beach, New Jersey, sort of a prep

school for Annapolis. That academy also had a couple of famous attendees: Moon Walkers: Alan Shepard and Charles Duke. NYMA was highly favored that day, but we were blown out.

On a furlough I was invited to visit my "swimming pool girl" Dorothy (Mickey) Lawrence and her mother in Queens. In my snazzy uniform, looking like a West Pointer, Mickey took me around and introduced me to her girlfriends and even had me play the piano. At least one of them, Jean Haulk, was "cute as pie" seemed impressed. She was one friend too many for Mickey because I secretly cut short my stay, took a room at a YMCA and spend some time with Jeannie Haulk. Later we wrote sweet letters to each other and soon, after back at the academy, I received a very affectionate letter, which began with a personal, tender love poem she said she'd been "inspired and had taken the time to compose just for me." I was thrilled, flattered and inspired to show it around to some of the guys:

> *How do I love thee?*
> *Let me count the ways.*
> *I love thee to the depth and breadth and height*
> *My soul can reach, when feeling out of sight*

It wasn't until much later that I learned her poem was written by Elizabeth Barrett Browning back in the 1850's! The more I've thought about it, strangely I can't recall ever having played a piano at the academy or even having seen one and I've wondered why. I <u>was</u> proud of my uniform and proud of being part of a great school, but was looking forward to the end of the year and was tired of the lack of freedom and privacy. My getting up early in the morning, taking orders from everyone and anyone, marching around, saluting, playing marches, marching and toting a rifle around, I never thought it was ever going to happen to me again. But I do believe the military training at NYMA helped me when I was later drafted into the army.

Bucknell University

Lewisburg, a small town about thirty miles from Bloomsburg, was the home of the Lewisburg Federal Penitentiary and Bucknell University. We weren't interested in the penitentiary so It would be Bucknell for me especially since my brother was already there and it was relatively close to Bloomsburg. But I made a dumb mistake and entered into the Chemical Engineering program. I'm not sure why I did except maybe it was because, as I mentioned before, I had always enjoyed chemistry when I was a kid. Most of the classes were way over my head... like trying to figure out how to use a slide rule, high math, numbers that didn't go up and down a scale...you name it and I didn't get it! Their music department wasn't so hot so I didn't want to change programs. I felt totally out of place at Bucknell.... subject wise and socially and I didn't look forward to being there very long. I was even beginning to miss reveille! It was, also around the time when my dad bought me a real old Chevy (or Ford) with a rumble seat. I was happy with it except it had mechanical brakes and every time, when it rained and I applied the brakes, the car would spin around in a circle!

During my first semester at Bucknell I lived in a second story room downtown in the house of a local minister. My part of the house was connected to his church and one day, up in my room, with the window open and making like Harry James on my cornet I heard: "Hey you up there!" Down on the sidewalk below   stood a rather thin pleasant looking rather studious young guy. "Pretty damn good trumpet," he said. "Come on down." His name was Warren Kistler and he became one of my best friends at Bucknell. Warren was a jazz pianist from Scranton, Pa. taking a business course. He played damn good commercial piano so we played lots of music together...me on the cornet and he on the piano. When I got tired of the church I moved into a men's dorm right down the hall from Warren. I thought it strange that every day guys would stop by his room for a minute. Why? It was to gaze at a picture frame on his desk facing the door. Each day, for everyone's appreciation, Warren would insert a different seminude photograph of some good-looking woman.

My other best friend at Bucknell was Jack Ireland, a tall, dark curly-haired, broad-shouldered, kind, loyal guy from New Jersey. Once we hitch hiked all the way from Lewisburg to his house and when we arrived it was fairly late and we were both pretty beat. After showing me my room I went right to sleep but suddenly, in the middle of the night, "*wham*" something hit me right in the middle of my stomach. It hurt and scared the hell out of me. He was his big tabby cat Jack had forgotten to tell me about.

One of the jobs I had for a while, to help with college, was working on the dishwasher at the women's dining hall. Before dinner Jack suggested I play the piano in the lounge so if some sweet coed came swaying by, sit on the bench or talk to us, Jack would be right there with a pad and pencil hoping to jot down her number for a date for us. Once in a while it worked! One day he received a sad telephone call from his dad

about his mother. She had been ill for some time
and had just died so he was told to come right
home. There wasn't time for traveling money, but
my mother and dad chipped in and got him on a
train right away. He left college, but we kept in
touch throughout the next few years. He had a
good job in Philadelphia with the 3M company and
later, when I in the army stationed at Fort Dix,
New Jersey, we were able to spend time together
again. Since he had an apartment between Philly
and Ft Dix, I was often able to stay there and
spend time away from the army post. Sometimes
we would search the newspapers to find a church
potluck to buy a good home cooked meal. After
the army we lost touch as I did with so many
other army buddies. I've wondered so often about
Jack Ireland, Warren Kistler, Jack Koch and all the
rest! Were they still around and where were
they? Would they remember me? But as time
speeds along it seems as though there's hardly
enough time for present friends. Later, when my
brother and I shared an apartment downtown in
the middle of Lewisburg, I met Velma Bob's

girlfriend who later became Bob's common-law wife. I also met Bob's friend Bud Lamade who lived down the hall and became another close friend. A story by itself because he was rich and weird!

Bud was a member of the wealthy Lamade family from Williamsport who owned the "Grit" newspaper. He was brilliant, somewhat chubby, wore glasses and looked like a white Forest Whitaker the movie actor.

He had a big old Packard car and enjoyed removing the tires, riding up and down the brick streets of Lewisburg in the middle of the night on the bare rims making a terrible racket. When I asked him why he did it he said "the people go to bed too early." Sometimes at night he'd place speakers from his window out on the roof. He'd turn the volume of his radio all the way up and wake up the sleeping neighbors. Since he probably paid the local police off frequently, he never saw a day of jail or paid a single fine.

Sometimes, when I went to visit him late in the morning or early afternoon, he'd be lying in his tub filled with large, almost overflowing soap bubbles. He had an attached board stretched across the tub and would lie there all day reading a book. One day when I went to his room, I found him sprawled out unconscious on the couch. I had been warned about this and had been given instructions. He had diabetes it was probably an insulin reaction, which meant an intake of insulin had lowered his sugar too much... so I ran to the kitchen, grabbed some sugar cubes and shoved them down his throat. He came to, was OK and was forever grateful. Though he had a habit of cutting classes to hunt or fish he always "aced" every test. Bud was a professional student who spent most of his adult life in some college or university. He not only held a Master's in English, but a Doctor of Medicine and a Law degree. The last thing I heard about Bud, from my brother, was that he had inherited the Grit newspaper and later died of diabetes.

Since my mild romances while at Military Academy I had had no new ones whatsoever but when my brother and I shared an apartment at

Bucknell I did have a crush on a lovely girl, a waitress at a local restaurant. It was disappointing at the time but funny when I think back.

Alone I went to lunch at a restaurant downtown one day and my waitress was a very lovely young lady... small and shapely with beautiful sweet lips and a "come hither" voice....a living doll! Love at first sight! I can't remember her name but I'll call her "Libby." I returned time and time again when I could when I knew she'd be working. Each time I tried to get the nerve to ask her for a date. (I think I was beginning to put on weight from going there so often) but still hadn't the nerve to ask Libby for a date. One morning, when I was sleeping on the sofa in the apartment and Bob was asleep in the bedroom, there was a knock on the door. I opened it and there stood my lovely doll Libby: " Is Bobby there?" she said.

Bob and Velma loved to dance, especially jitterbugging to a jukebox at the Moose Club in Milton (a small town just down the road from

Lewisburg.) One day an entertainment act was scheduled for the members of the local Moose Club and they needed a piano player. Bob, being a member, hired me to play but I wasn't told who or what to exepct: "Just be prepared to play "the Stripper, "he said." The night of the show, in the club's large meeting room, the guys all moved their chairs up in a semi circle, sat down and waited along with me at the piano. When the time came and I got the cue I started banging out the rhythm on this out-of tune old upright. In came a large pasties-breasted, skimpy "G" stringed, red haired, full blossomed woman. She teasingly danced around doing her burlesque thing for a while then slowly off came her pasties, one by one, flirting with this guy and that (shades of Tondeleo). I was still able to play the piano when swish.... off came her "g string." She was a red head alright, top to bottom! Then (I'm sure my brother put her up to this) she came over to the piano, sat on my lap rubbing my face between her boobs. I was semi paralyzed but never missed a beat. She kissed me on the cheek, got up and went into the <u>main</u> part of her act. Amazing! Still shaking her body, she cooed around one of the guys in the front and motioned for a lit cigarette, then moved back so everyone could get a good look. She began to smoke the cigarette and show the boys how versatile she REALLY was. She moved the cigarette to her navel, tightened the muscles and held it there for a moment. Then to the "oohs and ahs" of the all-male audience she bent way over, with her legs spread apart... then wider apart. Looking down, watching the action of her hand, she slowly, but oh so slowly, inserted the unlit part of the cigarette right below. Calling on some extra muscles, while the lit end of the cigarette protruded, she began to puff away! I flubbed the piano! Ah "Show biz!"

I was still in college and was at a party or something somewhere having a good time... until I spied this woman in an ugly print dress who was probably in her forties. She must have weighed at least two hundred and fifty pounds and was looking at me. I'll give her the name Martha (I'm not sure) and I don't remember where she came from or why she was there. Martha had long stringy hair, huge puffy cheeks so fat that I could barely see her eyes... just enough to see that now they were staring at me. That was only part of it for when she worked her way closer to me she smelled! She smelled bad! I moved further away and smiling an ugly smile, she flicked her tongue in an out and followed me like she was a predator and I was young meat she wanted to crush and eat for dinner. I eased my way into another room, searching for some kind of exit, feeling like I was back in time trying to close the garage and escape the "monster." Running into another room she followed giggling, enjoying the fun. I had some advantage because wherever I went so went the smell but how could anyone that fat move around so fast? It seemed as though most everyone had disappeared. Help! Maybe I was safe because I was in another part of the house but "oh no" so was she! Was there no escape? But then I saw a door which probably led to a basement and safety. As I hurried down the basement steps I hoped Martha wouldn't be somewhere behind. It was dark and jeeezzzz if she gets me down here what then? Suddenly in the semi-darkness, I smelled the smell and saw a large waddling shadow. Could there possibly be any enjoyment if she caught me? Looking around frantically I spotted a small open basement window but the smell now was about as strong as it could be and I heard hard loud breathing. I was trying not to imagine what it would be like if she caught me. *Do they arrest women for that?* If I could just crawl out that window, if I can't I'm going to be squashed male meat. For once I was lucky to be as short as I am, and was just able to squeeeeeeze through. If she tried hard enough to get through she might just break the wall down. She tried but got stuck in the window! The last thing I saw Martha her arms were flailing away and I was safely out running like hell!

Since they could now afford it, my mother and dad baled me out of Bucknell University and admitted me to the "Wills Eye Hospital" in Philadelphia to have an eye muscle operation on my right eye. It was considered to be THE eye hospital in the country with the best doctors. I had a comfortable room with a gentleman (and I'd never heard of this before) who was a Seventh Day Adventist. He was a nice man and didn't spout religion to me but I did learn that Adventists celebrated their Sabbath on Saturdays.

When it was time for the operation, I was taken to the operating room, locally anesthetized and had some kind of uncomfortable thing inserted in my right eye to hold the eye wide open. Nothing like today, I'm sure, because I was going to be awake the entire time. The operation was not only emotionally painful, especially because I had been hearing some sounds like "snip, snip." It was a fairly long operation and afterwards both eyes were bandaged so I couldn't see. There was a considerable amount of pain afterwards…. no great painkillers like those of today.

I was going to be there about a week and wanted some way to be occupied. Luckily there was a small piano in the hospital and the nurses knew I played. Every day one of them pushed me around, from floor to floor, up and down the elevators, to play the little piano for the other patients. One of the nurse's assistants was a girl named Mildred Hanck. (Here I go again) Mildred came to my room to feed me, read to me and just talk. She told me she was from New Hope, a suburb of Philadelphia, her family was devout Catholic and she wanted to become a nurse. Since my roommate was able to see, he kept telling me she was about five-four and how pretty she was. It was like listening to some character on a radio program and imagining what he or she looked like. I'm sure, from what I'd heard from the nurses and other patients that Mildred had great compassion and was excellent at her job. Also because of the amount of time spent with me, I felt she'd grown fond of me. She even had herself assigned extra time, particularly on my floor, to spend more time with me. After a while, when no one around, she would come sit very close and and me. I, not only was terribly grateful for her time and attention but was having another great crush. (*Hey I was just a dumb teen- ager*) And this time with someone I'd never seen. When the bandages were to came off Mildred held my and whispered, "I want my face to be the first thing you see." What suspense!

Not only was the operation a success but now, having been only able to feel her touch and hear her voice, Mildred was actually there and I never thought anyone could be so beautiful. My mother came to Philadelphia to stay a day or two when I was being dismissed from the hospital and it was arranged that Mildred would spend a day with us at the hotel. My mother, which wasn't usually the case, liked and admired Mildred, especially because she had taken such good care of me and seemed so dedicated. She and I continued to write and things went along status quo through the mail. I certainly hoped to see her soon again.

Music on the Road and Johnny Mehegan

My recent doctors advised me not to go back to school immediately and I was fortunate to be hired by "The Ed Harrington Trio" with Ed on the vibraphone, Harry Stevens on the bass and me on piano and vocals. It seemed strange because of having no drummer. Ed was a fairly short, thin nice looking guy with slick black wavy hair, a slight double chin and rather thin lips. I'm not crazy about vibes, but he was a damn good player. Harry was a fairly tall, somewhat heavy looking school teacher-like looking guy who wore glasses and was a reasonably good bass player...nothing great, but who kept good time and knew all the tunes. I never thought he liked me very much maybe because I thought he was kind of a bore. He would constantly point out something I already knew about and explain in detail. Like the time he called to my attention the breakwaters along the Chicago shore and explained their function endlessly. I got tired so of his unnecessary explanations that every time he would start about something I'd interrupt with "see those breakers out there?"

We were booked in Chicago and stayed in a fairly nice hotel, played pleasant jazz in one of the rooms at the Palmer House and left after our two week engagement. I don't remember much about Chicago except its having a bunch of bridges going somewhere or other, a train running around up in the air, someplace called the "Loop" and seeing Stumpy, Les Brown and Doris Day at the Sheridan Hotel. I didn't like Chicago too much then but then I didn't have a chance to get to know it well. I thought it to be a rather poor imitation of New York. *Most New Yorkers agreed.*

Our next booking was way down in Charleston, South Carolina and was to include a female vocalist. After some auditioning we hired a lovely voiced, sharp, young, good-looking woman with luscious wavy hair, smart clothes and who was a good pop singer....Bee Davis. The four of us, now "The Ed Harrington Quartet," with instruments and everything else all crowded into Harry's large middle-aged car and headed for

Charleston. Since we were wanted there to open as soon as possible we drove straight through. Away we went over the Smokey Mountains through hellish thunderstorms almost all the way. That was some struggle and a hell of an uncomfortable and tiring trip!

Upon arriving in Charleston we were put up in a pre-arranged hotel, got a good night's sleep and the next morning drove down town to the "Idle Hour Club" to meet the manager, give us the layout and get set up.   That nice gentleman was there but right in the middle of a sentence, in front of us, he fell over dead of a heart attack. It was not only a terrible thing and situation but there we were, contracted for a two-week engagement, in a state of shock and disappointment.   And after we'd broken our asses to get there.

In a way we sort of lucked out. The owner of the club was a nice understanding guy and told us although he'd have to close for a week he would give us a full week's pay and we could start the following week.   It was a sad situation but we were pretty beat and glad to have a paid vacation. I recall the one-way sidewalks in Charleston and the huge bridge, across the Cooper River, which went up and up so boats could sail under it...kind of scary. Since we had plenty of time on our hands Eddie warned about any female/male hanky- panky. "That kind of stuff can cause lots of trouble and break up groups." he proclaimed. A joke because <u>he</u> was the first to try to "hit on" our Miss Davis. But since Bee went for piano players, especially ones who had to find her right keys and arrange her vocals I was the lucky one. Hell, what else could I do? And although Mildred was on my mind, it wasn't much enjoyment or fulfillment having a relationship through the mails with her, especially when Bee was right there within arm's reach. Now was it? Especially since the time we were in Charleston we shared a room and spent most of our time together. Ed would have fired me except he needed me for the next job. Harry didn't give a damn but tried, as usual, to explain something or other to me. Of course there were no band break-ups except when the job was over.

I wasn't too crazy about Charleston; often couldn't understand the southern draw and thought the city was pretty slow moving. We performed on a small stage, had a good time playing for appreciative people who liked our music, a reasonably good sound system and lots of free meals. And Mildred? We were still corresponding, although less and less and I had my share of guilt because of Bee. After the three week engagement in Charleston, we headed back to New York to wait for the next job which was scheduled to be in West Hartford, Connecticut. They only wanted a trio especially since I sang and I was sorry to see Bee go. She headed back to Chicago to take another job and I was headed to Philadelphia to see Mildred. Then I received a letter that read something like this:

> *"My dearest Jack,*
>
> *My sister married a man who was non Catholic and there have been all sorts of problems between the two mostly because of*

their religious differences. It has caused lots of stress and friction in our family and has been a terrible time for all of us. My sister and her non-Catholic husband had a baby and are about to get a divorce. My mother's afraid, and says she'll do anything to keep it from happening again. She may be right. I care for you very much and have worried about this too. It's very hurtful but this is the last time I'll write and we can't see each other again. Please forgive me. Mildred."

I wasn't as upset as I should have been, but had a lot of mixed feelings, especially considering my escapade with Bee Davis. Since my Episcopal Church days, religion wasn't at the top of my controlling belief's list and has never been since. I've often wondered about the outcome if that Mildred relationship had continued. But that's not the first time or as they say: another "flash in the pan?"

While hanging around in New York, waiting to head to West Hartford, a friend told me about a great jazz piano player who was performing in New Jersey. His name was John Mehegan and it was suggested we go check him out...so we did. John was playing in a very crowded, smoky bar and the place was packed with jazz enthusiasts. At a medium sized grand piano sat this wiry, tall, serious looking guy with his long legs spread out under the piano, wearing a tweed coat, no tie, with his shirt collar underneath, turned up. And he was playing the hell out the piano....fast, furious runs, left hand a blur, changes of key, spread out "tenths" all over the keyboard. I closed my eyes and thought it was Art Tatum who most piano players, at the time, thought was the best. On a break my friend introduced me and told John I was not only a piano player too but also a great singer. Johnny sort of scoffed at the piano playing part but asked me to sing something. Since we both especially liked the Sinatra song "Nancy with the Laughing Face," he got my key; I took the mike, stood next to him, and sang. The crowd and John were pleased so he asked me to sing another which was "Try A

Little Tenderness." John and I got to be pretty friendly and later he became very important to me.

The Ed Harrington Trio headed, in Harry's car again, to West Hartford, Connecticut to the new job. It was in a lounge at a small ritzy hotel called "The Old Town Hall Inn," a fancy little place with a convenient diner attached. *I love diners!* We each had our own room in the hotel, small, compact, clean, fairly new and comfortable. There wasn't any dancing in the lounge so we played more jazz than usual. It was kind of a lonely time...another time in another city not knowing anyone. We were booked for two weeks and if they liked us we'd stay longer. Business was so good that the management decided to have continuous music...a good solo pianist to play between our sets. Immediately I thought of Johnny Mehegan and called him. He needed a change anyway and had just given his notice. He'd be up in a week since the money was good plus meals at the diner. He was especially glad since both he and his former wife were both from

Hartford. It was great having Johnny there, not only as a friend but someone from whom I could learn. Often, on my breaks, I sat next to him, watched and listened to him play. When he wanted to learn a classical piece the music was black with all the fingering marks. He carried small lap keyboard with springs on the keys, but no sound and when we traveled on a bus somewhere, Johnny would sit there... click, click, clicking away... with everyone staring at us. He seemed to know Leonard Bernstein very well because he often mentioned the word "Lennie" during a conversation. John was a strange but exceptionally talented guy with an oversized ego. He often said, as though it were an obvious fact: "there are only three great jazz piano players in the world...Art Tatum, Nat King Cole... and me!" At the time I thought he was right. Once he took me once over to his former wife's parents' house. His wife had once been a stripper which was hard to believe because she was rather short and kind of dumpy.... but very smart. The father was quite a collector...that is collecting pornographic books which filled his bookcases.

By this time I was tired traveling and playing with the trio and was anxious to finish college. Since the engagement had lasted quite a while I was also tired of listening to Ed's vibes, Harry's bass, my playing and singing and doing some of the same tunes over and over. Much of the time it was lonely and I remember, at Christmas time, having dinner in the Old Town Hall Diner by myself.

John knew I wanted to leave and told me about this wonderful Music Conservatory in Hartford "The Julius Hartt School Of Music." where he had once studied. (It later became part of Hartford University and is considered one of the best in the country). The Hartt school was especially known for its fine Opera Department. *(In the very earliest days of Television in* 1943, *Hartt presented the first, complete opera on television, Hansel and Gretel, (General Electric TV station, WRGB in Schenectady, New York) directed by Moshe Paranov.)* The school also had an excellent Piano Department and a first-class teacher of Composition, Dr. Isadore Freed. I made up my mind it might be just right for me. Besides, I enjoyed the city of Hartford.

I didn't see John again until several years later in New York City. He was alternating with the excellent Mary McPartland Trio playing at "The Village Vanguard" one of the best jazz lounges in New York. We were glad to see each other and he remembered and asked me again to sing "Nancy With the Laughing Face." I followed John's career that blossomed and bought one of his records: "How I play Jazz Piano." Later he had written a number of published, popular books on jazz piano playing and had been appointed head of the Jazz Department at The Metropolitan Music School. He had also held posts, as a lecturer, at Yale and Julliard. There was something I learned about John that was strange since many times I'd seen him coming on to women. In several books about Leonard Bernstein, I read John had been one of the many lovers of that great conductor-composer-pianist. A big surprise! One book described how Bernstein's wife Felicia ran from a party she was giving when she saw John arrive. Bernstein also dedicated a piano composition to Mehegan in his "Four Anniversaries" collection and the piece commemorates John's birthday, June 6, 1920. I can't think of Johnnie without including the following:

> The play "Street Car Named Desire" by Tennessee Williams had opened in New York and John had written the background music. Marlon Brando, the male lead (Stanley) in the play. had taken Broadway and New York by storm and was the talk of the town. The play, at various times, called for New Orleans Jazz which was performed live and piped in from a rather small room on the second floor of the theater.

One day John called and asked me if I'd like to come to the theater. Wow! There Johnny sat an old upright piano with three other musicians waiting for a buzzer to sound. Prepared to play, they waited until a light bulb went on. On went the light and they played the jazz until the light went off. It was, I believe at the end of an act that the door opened and in walked Marlon Brando himself, torn tee shirt and husky, humming and pounding rhythmically on a strapped on conga drum over his shoulder. John introduced me to Marlon, he smiled, shook my hand, mumbled something and continued playing. What an experience since he's always been my favorite actor and did the same part in the movie. My former friend and Lenny's…Johnny Mehegan died in 1984.

Julius Hartt Music School and Hartford

To be accepted into a music conservatory one usually must pass an audition. I got the go ahead from my parents who said they'd help foot the bill and I already had information from Bucknell sent to the Hartt School. I was able to secure an appointment with Moshe Paranov, one of the founders and the director. I was rarin' to go, but since playing only jazz for a long time, wasn't sure I'd have a shot at it.

Moshe Paranov was a dynamic, rather short, stocky gentleman, probably in his late forties, with straight black hair, a prominent nose, who sprayed saliva when he spoke. Someone wrote a poem about that once:

> *I once knew a fellow named Fritz*
> Who spoke with conspicuous spritz
> *Whatever he'd say*
> *Came out with a spray*
> *His sialoquent spurts gave fits.*

His studio was wood paneled, large and smoky from his pipe, on which he was usually puffing. In the center, as could be expected, was a large grand piano, stacks of music everywhere, plus the added presence of the Dean of the school, Professor Berkman.

Paranov, "Play something, whatever you'd like to play." Kimmell, "How about "Over the Rainbow" which I played, doing my share of improvising in kind of a classical style. A moment of silence...then he and Berkman laughed. Paranov, with a grin on his face: "That was quite a rendition but I really meant one of the classics...something by Bach or Beethoven, maybe Debussy." I proceeded to explain the amount of time between my earlier musical background and the recent jobs I had been playing.

Paranov: "Alright play a G major scale up and down three octaves like this." His fingers were a blur on the piano keys. I told them I hadn't practiced scales in years. Things were looking bad. Then Professor Berkman handed me a harmony exercise on a piece of manuscript paper.

Paranov: "We're in kind of a hurry now but we'll but give you half an hour outside. Do the exercise and bring it back." I looked at it for a minute, shook my head, paused and thought "what the hell," and played the entire exercise-chords and melody on the piano. Then another moment of silence before Dean Berkman finally spoke: "Hmm...that was pretty good." Paranov shook his head.

Paranov:: "Mister Kimmell, would you give us a moment and wait outside?" In about ten minutes they called me back. Professor Berkman told me it was obvious I had musical talent and Paranov agreed. Then I was told that, although it wasn't quite normal, they decided to give me an opportunity. I was handed a Beethoven Sonata, a piece by Debussy, and a book of scales. Paranov said. "Summer is coming up and you can practice here at the school if you want or anywhere else. Make sure we get the music back, learn as much as you can and return in a month and a half or so. Make an appointment and we'll see about it then for next semester." I stayed in Hartford, practiced my tail off at least four hours a day, and returned in a month. I wasn't great, but good enough to be accepted as a piano major.

Guess they thought they'd be able to fine-tune me.

When the next semester began, I shared an apartment, right across the street from a huge Insurance building first with a couple of guys and later with a great guy, Jimmy Mattingly, a Voice Major. The apartment was fairly large so we had our privacy. I enjoyed the school and the other students and it was definitely music and more music. The school, in the center of Hartford, wasn't a very large building, so sometimes there was a shortage of practice rooms... but I managed.

My piano instructor, Raymond Hanson, was a tremendously versatile pianist. Tall, husky, shorthaired blond of Scandinavian decent, he really had quite a story. During the Second World War he was a "conscientious objector" and was confined to duty in a hospital. Ray was certainly "patient" with me because I hated practicing. Another one of my courses was Composition. At one time or other I had written some music which showed some amount of creativity. My instructor,

120

Dr. Isadore Freed was a well-known, wonderful teacher having had David Raksin, a prolific film composer and the composer of the music for the movie "Laura," as one of his pupils. Composing came easy for me and was the subject I enjoyed the most and I realized I was pretty good at it. So did Dr. Freed. In fact I wrote so much music on the exercises given us that there hardly enough time to go over my music in class. Dr. Freed, having an empty hour after class, devoted some of it to me. One day, he took me by the hand and led me into Paranov's studio.

"This young man is my best student," he said firmly, "and I believe strongly that his major should be Composition not piano." My major was changed and it was the beginning of a very close friendship. I helped Dr. Freed copy a new opera he had just finished, "The Old Maid And the Thief," and we took many walks together discussing life in general and each other's music. When a piano piece of mine, called "Scherzo" was to be played at a concert and the pianist became ill, Dr. Freed wanted it on the program so much that he played it himself. He wasn't the greatest pianist in the world but did a pretty good job. (*I can still see him bouncing up and down on the piano bench with every accent in the music.*)

Once he told me he thought he would have had greater success as a composer if he had changed his name because it didn't sound so Jewish. He reminded me of some men in the arts such as: Harold Arlen, who was born Hyman Arluck; Gerorge Gershwin, born Jacob Gershowitz: and Irving Berlin, born Israel Isidore Baline. He suggested I use my middle name instead of "Jack." For the longest time, as a composer, I was "Normain Kimmell."

I was addicted to composing, which showed in my other grades, but it was always A+ in Composition. I wasn't playing cornet at all, but took some jobs playing piano whenever I could in downtown Hartford to help pay some of the bills. I didn't advertise my singing and often played with this one group who had a fairly good male singer who sang one particular song every night...and every night! Now whenever I see or hear the song "Garden In the Rain," I think of him and Hartford, Connecticut.

Many of my pieces were performed in concerts in the school and outside and I had some great and talented friends. One was Gilbert Johnson, who later became the first solo trumpet player with the great Philadelphia Orchestra. Gil, while practicing in a room, holding his trumpet nonchalantly with one hand, could play the most difficult orchestral trumpet solos. He was also a ladies man and was having an affair with the female secretary to Paranov. But that wasn't all the "goings on" in the school. The wife of Professor Berkman, who taught "Ear Training," was having an affair with Elemer Nagy, the lauded head of the Opera

Another one of my friends became the first oboist with the Montreal Symphony, and another was Virginia Copeland who played the soprano lead in the first performance of Menotti's 'Saint of Bleecker Street. Two other fellows I knew, not really close friends, who were exceptionally talented. One was Johnny Berkman, the son of the Berkman's who played jazz and was a double major in violin and piano. It's no wonder Irene; his mother was the Ear Training instructor. You could spread all your fingers out, slam them down on the keyboard and he could tell you every note. Years later I met him, after a performance, conducting the orchestra for an Ice Show and another time later conducting the orchestra for a show on Broadway about the Marx Brothers, called "Mini's Boys." The other friend was Erwin Zucker, another jazz pianist. He went to Los Angeles, changed his name to Jack Elliot and wrote arrangements and commercials for films. The last time I saw Erwin was back in Arizona. He remembered something he'd said to me years before when we were both at the Hartt School. It was about my Virginia Updegraff and Erwin remembered what he asked me then. "How's Virginia Phonograph? Have you given her the needle yet?" (*Though kind of crass I thought it clever both times.*)

Once a week we had a Master Class in the auditorium. Various students would perform
124

music (by memory) on the stage and be critiqued afterwards. I was to play, during one session Debussy's "Clair De Lune." It was the first time I'd ever been asked to play anything "classical" for a large audience and was so panicked that, when I began to play, my right leg was shaking so violently on the pedal, I was distracted and forgot the music. *Damn it, don't stop...improvise...improvise!* I did until I remembered where I was and continued to the end. The students laughed but applauded. Paranov, amused said: "I don't know how much Debussy would have enjoyed that, but you kept going, and enjoyed your "Debussyish Improvisation."

I haven't mentioned any romance lately and was usually too busy to do much dating but one day, at the Hartt School, I met Rubina Iacobucci, an organ major.

Ruby was a small, vivacious, strong willed girl with a pretty face that wanted to look Italian but didn't quite make it. Her family was from Prato, Italy. Hartford, at that time (and probably

125

still does), had a large Italian population and many of them were "Pratolons" meaning they were from Pratola, Italy. Ruby's mother, plump and spoke no English, was sort of their "Queen." She was very wise and if anyone of the "Paisans" needed help or advice, they came to her. The Iacobucci's were successful, had lots of money and owned a restaurant.

Ruby and I saw each other every day at school and drifted into a love affair. When I was neither attending classes nor composing, I'd be somewhere alone with Ruby or in her large house devouring fantastic Italian food. The first course: chicken and Italian soup and then spaghetti and then home-made meat balls served with wine from their large wine cellar. Then the meal would finish off with some delicious Italian desert and cookies from a huge barrow. There was so much food at the Iacobuccis they had two kitchens to serve it all. Most of the time there were other Paisans there and they always stared at me while saying something, of course, I didn't understand, and then they'd smile. There's no doubt I was feeling like part of the family and I believe <u>they</u> were feeling I would part of the family! An interesting family too.

Ruby's older brother Enzio was a hot tempered, short haired, Italian guy who was often in some kind of fight and in his third or fourth college. When I met him I think he felt he had to protect his sister. Since neither Ruby's mother nor dad could speak nor understand English I'd hear Ruby say, "Maaah," then continue in Italian. Mr. Iacobucci's restaurant/ pub was rather run-down but did a hell of a good business catering mostly to Italian "blue collar" workers. It was often suggested that he remodel his restaurant but he maintained if it was too 'capriccio" (fancy) he would lose business. A slight embarrassment for me was that I hated to practice the piano and my piano teacher Ray was married to Ruby's cousin Celia.

I can't recall, except this one time, what car I owned or my visits from Hartford to Bloomsburg. My cousin Gladys, my mother's sister's daughter from Monroe, Louisiana whom

I'd never met, came visiting to Bloomsburg just before I came for a day or two. She was a pretty, very dark-haired, slim girl, in her late teens or early twenties with a southern accent I could barely understand. She must have believed in "kissing cousins" and becoming familiar quickly because the first night she was there, and I was sleeping in the front room, she crawled in bed with me. After I'd gone back to Hartford, Ruby invited Gladys for a few days visit. Gladys must have had a strong prejudice toward Italians and a strong streak of jealousy because when she retuned to Bloomsburg she had nothing good to say about Ruby or her family. This caused problems between my mother and me and when Gladys left I was so upset I never wanted to see her again and didn't. I've always regretted that when she died some years ago. She and a son of hers, who was once the mayor of an Alabama City, were the only two relatives of my mother I ever met.

Besides spending time with Ruby I was writing a "Concerto for Piano and Orchestra,"

128

other piano music, many vocal pieces, a piece for piano and flute, and some band arrangements for my roommate Jimmy Mattingly who was always working. Jimmy was a good-looking guy, had lots of girl friends, was very easy to live with, and was a good pop singer. I worked very hard at school, but still didn't like practicing scales, playing Bach or spending time on the piano. Usually when I was at school I'd sit there with my bow tie on, composing or copying music. At our apartment, Jimmy and I and some other guys, would play Pinochle for hours, for money... sometimes all night. I was enjoying composing, Ruby, Jimmy Mattingly, school and my life in general in Hartford. Receiving my Bachelor's Degree in Music was in the very new future and I had already decided to stay another year to earn my Master's Degree.

My good friend Dr. Freed retired, for which I was sorry and I began some courses with a new composition teacher, Arnold Franchetti He was completely bald, had a slight German accent, and looked very much like a tall, angular, not so good-looking Yul Brynner. Franchetti worshipped the German composer Paul Hindemith and most of his references and examples seemed to begin and end there. I didn't like him as much but he was more progressive than Dr. Freed and was into Schoenberg, twelve-tone and atonal music. Once he demonstrated a kind of composition transferring the various heights of New York City Skyscrapers to musical notes on manuscript paper. This was all a rather new experience for me and I was glad for both teachers. One of his exercises was having us play a full orchestral score on the piano, many instruments in different keys. It was somewhat intimidating to me, especially since John Berkman was in the class and could play the score as easily as I could play sheet music. In a conducting class, I was told never to move the wrist around or signal out a player when he was about to play a solo. Since then, I've tried to notice this in prominent conductors and I've found that almost all moved the wrist and gave a cue to a soloist. I suppose another instance of learning a rule to break it.

My "Concerto for Piano and Orchestra" was the first work I had ever written for orchestra and as I've perused it again, realize it's really not a very good work. But it helped me later as my thesis, to receive my Master's Degree. First performed by the Hartt Symphony and Raymond Hanson was at the piano, it's in three movements: Andante Moderato-Allegro, Lento and Allegro Vivace and the score is 170 pages long. It would have been better if I had had a better piano technique.....able to compose a more interesting piano part. (*Otherwise should have practiced more!*)

In spite of Gladys, things seemed to be the same with Ruby Iacobucci. She was stimulating, devoted and other than her affection for me, quite level headed. But relations with her family and the Paisons were beginning to close in and also my roommate Jimmy Mattingly was beginning to fall for Ruby and it hardly bothered me at all. (*Was this a way out? Besides...*)

Young soft, small, girlish Virginia Updegraff came walking into the Hartt School one warm day for a piano lesson wearing a pink spaghetti strap dress that showed off, among other things, her magnificent virginal bosom. Gina (as she wanted to be called) was shapely, had very black rather short hair, a sort of delicate pug nose... she was lovely and reminded me of the actress Jennifer Jones. She was a number of years younger than me and about to graduate from high school. According to he, she'd had heard some of my compositions, admired composers, and was fascinated by jazz. And I admired pretty girls who looked like Jennifer Jones, played the piano, and were becoming interested in my roommate Jimmy!. I found myself making certain I was at school each time she came for a lesson and spent time with me and (please don't say it again) was losing interest in Ruby. *But oh how I hated to miss those wonderful Italian dinners!* I stuck around for a while longer but Ruby's possessiveness and the family things were getting too much and Jimmy, realizing how I felt, was becoming more and more caring for Ruby.

My real relationship with Gina began when she invited me over to her house for Sunday dinner and to meet her family. They were friendly (he was an insurance man) and seemed to be especially concerned about Gina. They seemed to like me and trust me and confided in me. It seemed, when Gina wasn't her usual vivacious self, she would become quite moody and seemed to wander around in another world. She played the piano beautifully...much better than I played "classical" music. Her fingers flew over the keys when playing a difficult Chopin "Nocturne." Once, at her house, I was playing some jazz on the piano and finished with a fast downward flourishing run. She asked why she couldn't hear the last four or five notes "like this," she said, as she played the same run for me just as fast, with every note crystal clear. Gina was brilliant and had a photographic memory and once we were on a bus and she was studying a new piece of music. When we arrived back at her house she played most of it for memory. I was now beginning to spend more and more time with Gina Updegraff and none with Ruby Iacobucci

But Jimmy Mattingly was now spending time with Ruby while Gina and I would be driving to Tangelwood to hear the Boston Symphony or going to the beach somewhere. Her mother and father kept on liking and trusting me which always surprised because I was older. When Gina was in one of her moods and disappeared somewhere, they'd call me and ask me if I would please find her.

Gina graduated from High School about the same time I received my Bachelor's Master's Degree from Hartt. I was at her graduation and she and her family attended mine, proud of us both, especially since a piece of mine, played at the ceremony said, "Dedicated to Gina" on the program. *No one from my family were there.*

Jimmy, and hopefully Ruby, were now in love and decided to get married in a small Catholic Church. Jimmy invited me to the service and it was a day in some ways I'd like to forget. I was sitting on the aisle near the middle and the

134

church was crowded with family and Paisans. When Ruby, looking beautiful in her wedding gown and Jimmy handsome in his tuxedo came down the aisle to the altar, angry eyes of the family and Paisans (with "you took all that time up and should have been the one" in their eyes) turned in unison and glared at me.

After graduating, Gina received a piano scholarship to the prestigious Eastman School of Music in Rochester, New York. I was glad for her, but concerned because I was familiar with the school-pressure of Eastman. Of course I was disappointed she'd be so far away. She was young and I knew she was probably lonely and vulnerable, especially in those surroundings. She would find someone else, which she did, and would have other interests in her life. We corresponded for a while, saw each other on her visits to Hartford, but our life took different directions, especially when I finished my Masters and was drafted into the Army. I saw her one more time, while I was on a furlough. A time that turned out to be a frustrating, memorable and rather comical event.   To make the story short:

After Jimmy had Ruby, Eastman School of Music and a boyfriend had Gina and the army had me, I visited a girl, Elaine, in Hartford and spent the night and next morning with her making out. After I left I called Gina to see how she was. She invited me over and, since her parents were out and after much reminiscing conversation invited me to her bedroom upstairs to finally consummate what we never consummated before. Two hot anticipating bodies together after all those semi-passionate, unfulfilled days and hours together in the past. Embarrassing moments followed. Of all the times to be tired and worn out from Elaine and fearful of Gina's family returning there I was.... shall we say incapacitated? What a masculine put down! One day, some years later, I called her mother and was told Gina had been married and had been in a hospital recovering from depression and anxiety. It was sad but I wasn't too surprised.

Ruby, during the time we still lived in Arizona; called two different times (somehow she found my number) sounding very drunk and sad. She had two children with Jimmy and they divorced. He'd become an alcoholic and died. Each time, when she called and learned I was still married, her conversation ended abruptly. It's extremely nostalgic and sometimes tragic learning later about people who, at one time or another, have been such a part of your life.

I'm In The Army Now!

I supposed I realized I must have been drafted into the army for my brains, certainly not for my body with its bad eyes and flat feet. It was the great Korean war and the army wanted college graduates as long as they could think, stand, breathe, walk, salute speak and take orders. So soon after I graduated the second time from Hartt with a Master's Degree, I was drafted. Since I'd been living in New England, I was sent to Ft. Devons, Massachusetts for processing. My first day there, I heard the word "motherfucker" for the first time, and I realized I was in another world and would be for two "mother fucking" years. At Devons only a couple days, I was physically examined, stuck with needles and given a uniform that said "soldier" all over it. Soon I was to be bused down to Ft. Dix, New Jersey, for Basic Training. I was no longer Jack Normain Kimmell, "brilliant" composer, but was now Private #US51091666, US Army!

I called Alice Michalaras, a dear friend from school, and told her the busing schedule, and an approximate time we'd be making a rest stop in West Hartford. Alice was there was a carload of my friends from school who give me a grand sendoff helping to raise my spirits. At least it wasn't such a bad beginning.

Ft. Dix was a huge army camp close to Trenton, New Jersey. Its sole function was to destroy individuality, teach how to march, obey orders, and kill the enemy. We were housed in huge long wooden barracks filled with rows and rows of cots and footlockers. The "head" (bathroom), that gave us absolutely no privacy, was what I hated the most. Because of my military academy experience things came pretty easy but I schemed to make things easier for myself. Since many lineups were alphabetical, I was next in line to Warren Krupp, also a college graduate. Warren and I decided, when there was a roll call for some kind of duty, whether it was best to be at the head, middle, or end of the line. Sometimes on "sick-call," I'd stop somewhere and go to sleep. My outfit would think I was at the Infirmary and the Infirmary would think I was back with my outfit. Sleeping wasn't difficult because we were always up around five in the morning, falling out for the mess hall, tired but getting ready for the new day's hell.

I crawled on all fours under barbed wire and live machine gun bullets, marched with full pack, wearing a heavy steel helmet, slept in a tent in the mud, marched around shouting all those things you see in movies, and obeying permanent army assholes.

I shot a rifle grenade for the first time and the kick of it knocked me down. Another time I was so scared throwing a live hand grenade that I threw it into a huge mud puddle spraying everyone around with mud. Some of the officers were unlikable bastards and I was sitting on the end of a bench in the mess hall one day. This nasty lieutenant, we particularly disliked, walked by with his food tray. I reached my foot out and tripped him causing a mess in the Mess Hall. Of course it was an accident! He didn't enjoy it but for a few minutes I was a hero.

Memoir of a Musician

Since I have almost no vision in my right eye and M1 rifles are made for right-handers with the bolt on the left side, I had to learn how to shoot left handed, reaching over across to operate the bolt. It was clumsy but I became a pretty good shot. During the six weeks of basic raining we were not allowed to either be away from the camp, or visit any recreational facility. The first day, afterwards, I found a service center on the base and in one of the rooms was a record player and a recording of Tchaikovsky's Sixth Symphony. I was alone and listened as though I'd never heard it before. I remember being so moved that I could feel the tears rolling down by face. It seemed as though the music was a bridge to my former world.

Since "trumpet" was listed as part of my records and because there were so many other trumpet players I was given an "MO" (Military Occupation) for baritone Horn instead. I was sent over to the 9th Division "Band Training Unit" where bandsmen were trained militarily and somewhat musically. Upon graduation they were

141

then sent to Korea, Germany and any other place they were needed. (in combat they were usually stretcher-bearers.)

I was as rebellious as I could get away with in the army and continued to be in the hundred and fifty piece marching band. I paid guys to clean my horn, polish my shoes and it was rare when my locker passed inspection. I lucked out because there was a sergeant in the company who had studied at the Hartt School who was extremely protective. He warned if I didn't "shape up I'd be shipped out."

Our commanding officer was Warrant Officer Dominque Gaudette, a rather medium sized, stocky, mustached gentleman whose talent was anything but music. Once outside, when he was conducting the Star Spangled Banner, an airplane flew overhead and while staring up at the plane, he continued waving his baton completely out of rhythm. One of his fortes was inspecting the bottom of our boots. Once, when I had a slight hole in the bottom of my right boot, he was inspecting and it was my turn, I showed him the bottom of my left boot. Then I then turned around backwards and showed him the bottom of my left boot again. Ok Private Kimmell!

One day I lucked out. A strange box was sent over one day from the Signal Corps. It was some kind of contraption that could reproduce messages. Nobody knew how or what to do with it. We needed lots of copies of music for the growing band and I got the bright idea that it just might somehow do the job. I got permission to spend two days finding the directions, figuring it out and getting the necessary materials and paper. By the end of the second day I was able to reproduce an endless supply of music. Gaudette loved it! Gaudette loved me! "Instead of being shipping out this guy, I'm going to make him part of my permanent "Cadre" of fifty." Private Kimmell was now the official baritone horn player in the newly formed concert band and would be permanently stationed at Ft. Dix. *Ta ta ta ta ta ta Ta !*

Although Gaudette was the commanding officer, Sergeant Kuhaut, a gruff, tough, somewhat pocked-faced looking "regular army" guy, conducted the concert band. Although he kind of looked like a gangster, he did have an unexpected sensitive way about him and was a fair musician. But since the concert band was comprised of excellent selected musicians, mostly college graduates, it created a problem… compounded by me. When his conducting or interpretation of the music was not as I (or others) thought it should be, I would kind of glare at him or look up at the ceiling slightly shaking my head.

Since the band would be performing some concerts in public Gaudette (somehow thinking I could do most anything) asked me if I would design the front of our music stands. I did it… he liked it… and the music stands were painted. (This all produced for me no marching around and picking up cigarette butts time). With hints here and there Gaudette was wise enough to see the problems with Sgt. Kuhaut because the sergeant was shipped out to somewhere in Texas. Upon the suggestion of my Hartt School sergeant friend,

144

the knowledge of my credentials, the general consensus of the band and being in Gaudette's good favorite, I was promoted to Corporal (and acting Sergeant) and named the conductor of the 9th Division Band.

My remaining time in the army was better than I could have ever hoped. In a small building near the barracks, with a piano, I could arrange and compose. I composed an original theme for the band's weekly performance on early Dumont television and among other things, wrote a transcription of Gershwin's "American In Paris" and part of a Symphony for band. Each Friday afternoon a bus picked us up and took us to not far away Philadelphia to watch and hear Eugene Ormandy conduct the Philadelphia Orchestra.

A somewhat effeminate, chubby guy with straight black hair (always combed immaculately) Sergeant Richard Barrows was our First Sergeant. Although he had been drafted, Richard, because of his excellent clerical skills and office management, was quickly promoted to first sergeant. In civilian life he was also the organist and choir director of his church in upper New Jersey and there I was...the resident composer. Richard commissioned me to compose an Oratorio from words of Milton's "On the Morning of Christ's Nativity" and was decided to be written for chorus, organ, piano and tympani.

I was given plenty of time to compose it and the completed music was copied and sent to the choir. We were to drive up for a quick rehearsal and the performance. It was a night of one of the worst snow storms of history in New Jersey and Richard, the timpanist; pianist and I arrived two hours too late. The concert was cancelled, we were all disheartened, and I was only able to hear parts of it later.

Romance, or whatever... for a change during those two years, was rather insignificant. It wasn't easy to go to a dance and be singled out by some great chick when there were so many of us, we all wore the same uniform and wore glasses and many were better looking than me. I certainly didn't fit the mold of the "hell bent for leather," big, tall, handsome, motorcycling type
146

guy they were probably looking for so when I went to a service club all the bussed in girls looked right passed me by. But there were a few memorable "interesting" experiences:

When I could get home to Bloomsburg, sometimes I might call this very nice Rosemary Toth. She was pretty and sweet, dark curly haired, easy going and was an anesthetist assistant I enjoyed her company except her hair always smelled of ether. Every time I'd lean over to kiss her goodnight I'd become dizzy and once almost fell sleep in the car.

A young lady I met at a dance did like me enough to invite me for a visit overnight at her home. We were sitting on her porch swing doing a little mild hoochee-cooing when she said, "Jack, I want to be honest with you. If or when you finally get there, what you think you're feeling is not all me... I'm wearing "falsies.""

I had a buddy, Joe Danko from Ohio who was a hell of a good tenor sax player. His main topic of conversation was the great jazz sax player Stan Getz, whom he worshipped. Joe spoke often of his hometown, Masury, especially the fact that there were so many bars next to each another up and down the streets. Our company was on leave for a few days, I had a car, and Joe invited me take the long drive to his home that was just over the Pennsylvania border. I never saw so many bars. Joe had mentioned this girl, Barbara who he wanted me to meet…. a friend of his wife. Barbara was one of those girls, so pretty, that you couldn't stop staring at her. There was a piano at Joe's house and during the next couple of days; we spent time with the two girls, playing jazz, yakking and generally having fun. I felt a strong attraction between Barbara and me from the beginning, but of course, there was a boyfriend. My last night in Masury, Barbara had an early date with the guy at her house that evening. And the plan was this: she'd encourage the boyfriend to take an early leave and I was to wait in my car, on top of a hill, overlooking the house, and watch until he drove away. I waited…and waited some more! His car was still there…I waited….and waited….no doors opened...the car was still there, then the lights went off! I'm outta here and I never saw Barbara again. Oh what the hell!

I met many good guys and good musicians in the army band. One trumpet player was Eugene Blee who later became the first trumpet player with the Cincinnati Symphony. Another was clarinetist Bob Weber who gained fame as a Dixieland clarinetist. It's sad to realize that I never saw or heard from any of the guys again other than Dick Burrows a year or so ago. Maybe we all wanted to put it out of our minds and jump back into our previous lives. It could have been two years wasted but I don't think it was and I consider myself very fortunate and somehow think I was important.

When I received an honorable discharge from the Army on August 28th, 1956, I received several letters of commendation. One was from the Commander of the 9th Infantry Division, Major General Roderick R. Allen. I have copied them below:

Training inspectors from Headquarters First Army have rated Band Instruction, directed by you, as Superior during the inspection conducted 29 April to I May, 1952.

I should like to take this opportunity to commend you for this outstanding performance of a very important duty. Your attention to duty in this commendable manner not only reflects the highest credit upon you, but is also in keeping with the highest traditions of the United States Army.

I exhort you to continue this superior performance of duty as a fine example to all military personal of the highest standards desired by the Ninth Infantry Division.

Another from Dominque Gaudette, Commanding. CWO USA Bandleader:

It gives me great pleasure to offer this expression of appreciation to Cpl. Jack N. Kimmell with whom, as a member of my band, I have been closely associated for almost two years. During this association, Kimmell

*performed in almost every
conceivable capacity: conductor,
bandleader, instructor, arranger,
vocalist, accompanist, copyist,
composer, and instrumentalist. In
all these assignments he has
never given less than his best,
and in so doing, he unwittingly
transmitted this devotion to duty,
youthful enthusiasm, and sincerity
of purpose to his peers.*

*On a number of occasions,
to cite one example, he is known
to have worked through the night
on an original composition or on
the copying of parts that were
needed the next morning.
Because he "did the job" without
commotion, rancor, or reward, it
may have seemed to be taken for
granted. One of the purposes of
this letter is to acknowledge now
my personal gratitude for the
diligence and devotion which Cpl.
Kimmell accomplished his diverse
assignments, some of which must
have been personally aggravating
and musically unrewarding.*

*It is a source of keen
satisfaction to have observed that
as a result of his military
experience which frequently
makes supreme demands on the
individual - emotionally, physically*

and intellectually - Kimmell has matured as a musician, and as a person. I have no doubt that he will achieve outstanding success in civilian life in whatever musical field he chooses to pursue.

I should like to single out for particular mention Cpl. Kimmell's conducting ability. In the past year he has been conductor of our Concert Band. The band's appearances on the Dumont Television Network and the WCAU and WFIL Radio Network, for instance, under Cpl Kimmell's direction have been must praised by audience and producers alike. Subsequent invitations to play return engagements bespeak their favorable reception. His command of the baton, his ability to penetrate into the core of a musical score, and then translate his interpretation to the musicians under his baton is certainly most praiseworthy.

In conclusion, I should like to reiterate, in the name of Service, my appreciation for the selfless, whole-hearted cooperation Cpl Kimmell has extended to our Band during his tour of duty. I sincerely believe that, as the result of this, music in the Army has profited by the association.

Dominique Gaudette
CWO USA Bandleader
Commanding

HEADQUARTERS 9TH INFANTRY DIVISION

TO: Whomever It May Concern

1. Corporal Jack Normain Kimmell who, because of his initiative, perseverance and ability, has most successfully directed the 9th Infantry Division Band for the past few months, will upon re-entering civilian life this week leave a position that will not readily be filled.
2. His cooperation with this section has done much to foster good public relations between this post and the surrounding communities through the activities of the Division Band.
3. I consider it a most pleasant duty to give him my sincere recommendation.

Walter C Carroll, Jr.
Major, Arty
Public Information Officer

*HEADQUARTERS 9TH INFANTRY
DIVISION ARTILLERY, Fort Dix,
N.J. 13*

> *TO: Cpl Jack N Kimmell, US
51 091 666, 9th Div. Band, Ft.
Dix, New Jersey*

*1. Forwarded with gratification.
Duty performed meriting official
commendation   is the acme of
satisfaction. Keep up the fine
work.*

*2. A copy will be placed in your
201 file.*

> *G. S. Beurket Colonel Arty,
Commanding*

Midland, Michigan State University and Marriage

All during my time in the army I contemplated studying for a Doctorate in Composition at the University of Heidelberg in Germany. Why? I'm not quite sure, except I heard it was the university for a composer. However I didn't know or like the German language and realized the difficulty and was way too far away. Since I needed some time to figure out what to do next, brother Bob, who was living in Midland, Michigan with his family, invited me to come stay for a visit, get the army out of my head and decide what to do next.

Midland, Michigan was the home the huge Dow Chemical Co. (I could sure tell by the smell!) Bob and Velma's house was small but cozy and although there were kids, Penneye and Donna Jean, I was able to have my own room. Velma was pregnant again at the time and was an attractive, happy go lucky lady, a great cook who enjoyed parties, playing cards and of course dancing. I guess she liked me okay and also realized I helped financially by contributing money

I'd saved and was receiving from army benefits.
One of my favorite enjoyments was going to bed
late at night, turning on my small portable radio
and listening to Jean Shepherd's stories from
Cincinnati. *Later he also wrote a movie "A
Christmas Story" that's played every Christmas.*

Bob, following in our mother's footsteps
had opened a dance studio. He was also
employed by Dow, which had its own Music
Department directed by Ted Vosburg. It was an
important part of the community and sponsored
concerts in their auditorium, performed musicals,
and maintained an all male chorus, at the time
was one of the best and most famous in the
country, a hundred male voices all employees of
Dow. Because of his theatrical skills, Bob was
given a job directing shows, designing scenery
and choreographing dancing.

Ted heard some of my music and
commissioned me to write several arrangements
for his men's chorus: "Surry With the Fringe On
Top." and compose a ballet to be called "Phenique
Synthique" which was supposed to illustrate, in

dance, the chemical evolution of Phenol one of the company's main products . *Pretty far out!* I wrote the music for two pianos, a number of ballet dancers and Bob danced the part of the main chemical." It was performed and led to several more of my compositions being performed, including a piece for cello and piano and some vocal music. All went well at Dow except one day. After visiting my brother in one of the buildings on the second floor, I was in a hurry to rush down the steps and leave. Believing the large opening was open to the outside I ran and crashed into a large spotless glass door, knocking myself silly onto the floor.

When Bob was rehearsing and directing the musical "Finian's Rainbow," I met a lovely blond, blue-eyed young soprano, Mary Eleanor High, who was doing one of the leads. I spent some time at rehearsals, admiring her singing, and admiring Mary Eleanor. We had some dates, nothing serious but I enjoyed seeing her house because of the curved driveway and the tall white pillars in front like Greek architecture. Mary Eleanor was lots of fun except when she reiterated all her endless ills. According to her, there wasn't a disease that had passed her by. It made me feel she was too fragile to touch and I hardly did! If you asked her a question, she'd pause and roll her pretty blue eyes then manage, somehow, to insert some illness into the answer. She told me her father, who was a doctor, had committed suicide but I never found out if it was true. I did have a scare. A few years ago I received an email from an unknown woman and I don't how she found my email address, but I know it's not too difficult these days. The woman lived in Bay City (not too far from Midland) and wanted to know if I was the "Jack Kimmell" who once knew her mother years ago. I had and... very well. She wrote that her mother was married to a nasty man who was also an alcoholic and there was some doubt about "who her real father was." I wrote and told her yes I was the Jack Kimmell who had known her mother years ago, but didn't go into the "Father" thing and waited apprehensively for her next email. Fortunately I never heard from her again!

In Michigan, of one resides for at lease six month period,, which I had, it would lower the cost of college tuition in the state. Also as a former G.I, I had financial help from the government. I was still anxious about the Doctorate in Composition so I contacted the University of Michigan and Michigan State College. Only Michigan State, in Easy Lansing, (which later became Michigan State University) offered the degree and it had just been recently instituted. After sending my college and army records and some compositions to Dr. H. Owen Reed, head of the Composition Department and an appointment was arranged.

Dr. Reed was a pipe smoking, handsome, dapper gentleman, probably in his late thirties or early forties. I knew he was a well-know professor, scholar and composer with a PhD from Eastman School of Music in Rochester, was a contemporary of Leonard Bernstein and had written one of the most famous works for band:

"La Fiesta Mexicana." He was enthusiastic, exceptionally pleasant, and had studied my records, liked the compositions, and was encouraging. I was told, if approved, there would be many requirements: lots of classes, including language, straight "A's" in Composition, a large musical work (my Doctoral dissertation) and oral exams. If I met all the requirements the degree would be a PhD. Soon after, I received the news that I'd been accepted. Happily I was headed for East Lansing and Michigan State College (later University) to become one of their first two Doctoral Candidates in Composition.

My classes included: Composition, Conducting, Musicology, German, Orchestra, Theory, 16th Century Counterpoint, Television, History of music, a Symphonic work, Dramatic writing, History of Theater, Acoustics and Contemporary American Theater. Dr. Reed made arrangements so, instead of the German language, I could create visual music charts and pass a French reading exam. For the French exam I hoped I'd remember enough from high school.

I didn't so I hired a tutor and passed it the second time.

The football team was a big thing, especially because of the rivalry with University of Michigan and the Rose Bowl competition. The football band shows seemed to be almost of equal importance. Leonard Falcone, a well-known bandleader and baritone player was the band director but was definitely from the old school so Dr. Reed suggested I write special arrangements for the hundred and fifty piece band. I did spending many hours for mostly glory and little pay. I rented an apartment in Lansing, earned extra money playing jazz down town and commuted to East Lansing for classes.

The Drama Department was to present the old classical play "Medea" and I was commissioned to write background music. During rehearsals I met and had a several dates with the choreographer Pat Jones who introduced me to her roommate, Nancy Morrison a dancer in the play. Nancy's story was quite a story. She had recently been married but dropped out of school soon after her marriage. Her new husband suddenly died of Polio now she was back in school. Nancy and I began to date after the rehearsals of "Medea." but Pat warned me to be very careful with Nancy's feelings because of her recent tragedy.

One day, I because I was having a serious bout with pneumonia, although Nancy was expected to go home to Dearborn, she decided to stay and take care of me. I was having an attack of shivering and Nancy was in bed with me trying to keep me warm. Suddenly the unlocked door opened and in walked Nancy's father. Obviously he was especially concerned about her. There was anger on his face and terror in his heart. "Why hadn't you told mother and me you weren't coming home and what the hell are you doing here in bed with HIM?" "He's sick with pneumonia and I'm keeping him warm." I gathered some strength and shouted: "I'm sicker than hell and she'sssss keeping me warm and don't worry, I'll marry your daughter!"

We did get married not too long after and had a lovely wedding reception in downtown Lansing. Then I did one of the most ridiculous things I've ever done. It was a Saturday and Michigan State was about to play an important football game at the stadium. I'd written the special arrangements for the band's halftime show. Soon after lunch I suddenly arose and announced I had to leave and hurry to the stadium. I arrived just in time to hear: "The arrangements for the Michigan State Band are by Jack Normain Kimmell." I've often wondered if that's where our marriage began to slowly go down hill.

We moved to a larger furnished apartment in East Lansing, rather close to the band practice field and it was rather enjoyable hearing my music as we ate breakfast or lunch. The football team won the Big Ten Championship that year and was headed for the Rose Bowl in Pasadena along with the band, my arrangements and Nancy and I. We traveled on a special train sponsored by Oldsmobile and there were a number of stops along the way. I marched, in uniform, along side the band and my arrangements were played in a number of cities along the way. The football team won the Rose Bowl that year against UCLA, my music was a hit. As a matter of fact Dr. Reed informed me that several west coast band leaders were fired because of there "inferior " band arrangements.. I was there one more time arranging for the band which included an original composition "Toy Town Band On Parade" which included toy bells and toy trumpets.

Before entering school for my doctorate and since I'd been in the army and away from the academic world, I had feared my subjects would be difficult for me, especially since I witnessed the fate of several others. But I had no problems, especially in Composition and even took over a few of Dr. Reed's classes when he had to be away. He and I had great sessions together. He was a great champion and not only enjoyed my compositions, but also my piano playing and singing. That appreciation created a small rift between the Composition department and Vocal

164

department. Dr. Reed had recently completed an opera "Peter Homan's Dream" and considered me just right for the part of Peter Homan. Since the Vocal department thought it wouldn't be proper for a Composition major to sing the lead instead of someone in their department we decided it wasn't worth the trouble. So instead I played the piano in the orchestra.

About this time I met Kathi Swets and her husband, Adrian who became my dearest of friends. I was playing with several groups in downtown Lansing, one time or another to earn extra money while at school. One happened to be a "Mickey Mouse" group that but paid well but I didn't enjoy. One evening, after finishing a set and stepping down from the band stand, this lovely young blond lady, sitting at a table with another lady, motioned me over, complimented me, wondered what I was doing with this group and asked me if I gave piano lessons. Quite taken back by her exuberance how could I say "no'? I would teach at her home since I had no piano. Kathy had a terrific ear, but wanted to learn more chords and technique, and couldn't have been a better student.

The Swets lived in a rather small house in Lansing and had two little girls, Debby and Heidi. I was introduced to Adrian and eventually introduced them to Nancy. Adrian and Kathy were both originally from Grand Rapids, Michigan, Adrian having had a degree from Michigan State University. He now owned a Roofing and Siding Business, why.... I don't know because he was brilliant and talented as a writer. One memorable afternoon we decided we would see who could write a song with words quicker, the two ladies or Adrian and I. I think they just beat us. Their song was a jazzy "My Guy Is Ivy League," and ours was a comical "Boom Boom Mama's Back In Town." Nancy and I spent many wonderful times with Kathy and Adrian n the beaches at Lake Michigan and several trips to Quebec. It was the beginning of a wonderful friendship for me that has continued throughout the years, as they became my closest and dearest friends.

Married Life and the "Big Apple"

Things were happening that began to pull Nancy and I apart and at the same time I had a strong desire to take a vacation my completing my PhD. and write an opera. The name Jean Karsavana, who lived in New York City, caught my attention in some operatic literature I read. She had not only written the libretto to an opera by Lukas Foss, "The Jumping Frog of Calavaras County," but had written an English translation to an opera by Prokofieff. Seemed to be excellent credentials so I called her in New York City, elaborated on myelf and she was interested. There was only one catch. Moving to "the Big Apple" takes a lot of money!

It was suggested, with most expenses paid, that we live in Dearborn with Nancy's family for the summer, get a job and make some money. Nancy spoke to her dad who got me a job and suddenly I was working at a large factory, in a small wooden building, handing out tools. How efficient I was... and everything catalogued and in perfect order. And wearing a hard hat that wasn't military issue!

Nancy's mom and pop, who were wonderful to us, gave us a car to use, treated us to Tiger baseball games and actually seemed happy we were there…even me, especially when I played their old upright piano. We were able to get away on weekends and once drove to my nostalgic old stamping grounds in the Poconos. It was sad though because things had changed. The large famous resort "Buck Hill Falls," had seen better days, "Pleasant Ridge House" no longer existed, being a victim of a fire, and the Log Cabin store, where I courted Betty Anglemire, was a junky gift shop. It was almost too difficult to handle!

Having saved up some money, at the end of the summer, we were off to New York where we rented a second story furnished apartment. It had a black and white checkered-board floor, was on Jane Street in the Village and right down the street from Jean Karsavana.

Jean was a tiny, ethnic looking middle-aged Jewish woman with a slight limp and a breathing problem because of having only one lung. She was a widow, a workaholic, brilliant and spoke with a slight crisp accent. Her knowledge of literature was amazing and she lived in a quaint, very old wooden, narrow, three story house with a beautiful Siamese cat she adored. We grew to have great affection for Jean and Siamese cats.

The plot for our proposed opera was to be an adaptation from a sad short story, "The Birthday Of the Infanta," by Oscar Wilde. It was mostly about a twelve year old Spanish Princess and an ugly Dwarf. I was somewhat apprehensive about the subject matter because it wasn't contemporary and I wrote contemporary music. Jean had already begun the libretto and I got to work on the music... page after page, even including an orchestra score. I gradually sensed that Jean's libretto was too frothy, archaic, wordy...and I suppose for lack of a better word "old fashion." Though I had spent hours writing I was discouraged and uninspired and gave up. The many pages sit home in a large envelope in a cabinet!

Nancy and I were taking advantage of the New York Theater scene whenever possible. When Kathy and Adrian Swets came to visit us once we saw Frank Loesser's "The Most Happy Fella." Nancy and I also saw the world premier of Samuel Barber's opera "Vanessa," which was quite extravagant but which I thought was over written and much to do about little. In the meantime I was using material from my "Medea" music writing a "Suite from Medea" for instruments which won a Michigan Composer contest. As life went on in the big city, Nancy had an excellent job working for the New Yorker magazine. One of her co-workers was Karen Hansen of whom Nancy became very close friends. As did I!

Karen Hansen, tall, slender and attractive, was a young lady with a sharp mind and a quick wit. She was from a wealthy Danish family who were involved in shipbuilding and had a lovely home just north of New York and traveled to Denmark once a year. Karen was a hell of a lot of fun and grew interested in me as Nancy grew interested in Karen's her tall, blond, handsome
170

brother who grew interested in Nancy. There we four were in the "Big Apple!" Nancy and Karen's brother... and Karen and me...two lovely ridiculous couples! Karen was even caring enough to give me a big birthday party at her house. I was at a lavish party with Karen and about twenty people, none of whom I'd ever met before, minus my wife who was with Karen's brother.

Karen enjoyed spending money on me and once she <u>took</u> me to an expensive Danish restaurant. We had a marvelous Danish dinner and got very tipsy on a Danish vodka-like drink, Akvavit and a cherry tasting liqueur called "Peter Herring." I was really feeling it and after dinner we walked hand and hand recklessly down the middle of a New York street to a theater where we necked in the balcony to the movie "The Bridge On the River Kwai." When Karen's family was away and Karen was alone once she invited me to her house for the evening. When I returned home to our apartment later that evening, Nancy gave me hell for not staying all night with Karen. She reminded me the house was rather secluded and I shouldn't have let Karen alone. So much for a happy marriage!

Nancy and I moved to a terrible apartment on Elizabeth Street, near the Bowery. We moved in and quickly moved out leaving my piano there for ever more for some reason or another. In the meantime Jean K's Siamese cat had kittens and we were given two beautiful ones which we named "Yum Yum" and "Black Balls." I finally decided I'd had it with New York apartments, operas and the ridiculous situation with Nancy and Karen and I'm sure Nancy agreed. By this time she had temporarily moved in with Jean, Karsavna and though I loved New York, it was a good time to go back to Michigan and finish my degree. By this time Adrian had transferred his roofing and siding business and family to East Grand Rapids. Since we all thought it was time to write our musical we decided I would stay with the Swets' and commute to East Lansing and Michigan State. Off I headed off to Grand Rapids, with my Siamese cat "Yum Yum to write a musical, hope for possible glory and finish my Ph.D

The subject of our musical would be... *guess what?* The roofing and siding business. Adrian got to work on the libretto and I got to work with Dr. Reed on my doctoral thesis. We decided it would be large composition for symphony orchestra work and wind quintet: Flute, Oboe, Clarinet, French horn and Bassoon.

Soon after returning on February of '59, I was introduced to Mary Powell, a lovely blond woman with three children (Chuck, Mimi and Mike) sitting near the Swet's spinet piano in their den on Briarwood. I was told she had heard much about me and suddenly I had this warm feeling. When we were alone for a moment I remember saying: "Do you feel something in the air going back forth between us?" (It wasn't just a line, I really felt it.) Mary Powell was not only beautiful but gifted with an amazing beautiful mezzo soprano voice and a great musical sense. She and Kathy had met while both were doing the musical "Finian's Rainbow." There was something in the air all right but it was the beginning of many future complications since Mary was married to Bert Powell, had three kids and I was still married to Nancy. (*You must be thinking* "*not again.*")

Adrian had transferred his roofing and siding business to Grand Rapids. It worked this way: One of his workers would go out (canvass), find a house that looked like it could use a new siding job, knock on the door and try to make an appointment for Adrian to come back in the evening to sell the deal. Since I was living under their roof receiving their hospitality one day I said: "Hell, I could do that for you. Why don't you let me try?" One afternoon in February, driving and looking around for "the house." I found one, I rang and a nice lady opened. "How do you do," says I, smiling at the woman while glancing into the room noticing a piano. "I'm representing a roofing siding company and notice the outside of your house could use some fixing up." Before she could respond or slam the door, I said, "Hmm, that' a nice looking piano you have. Do you play?" "A little" she said. Why do you?" Smiling, I said, "Yes, I 'was a music major in college."

"Oh my" she said, "Would you like to try it?" I did, I played, she listened, smiled and offered me a piece of cake and cup of coffee. I made an appointment for Adrian for the next evening and he sold the deal!

I kept busy playing jobs in about every hotel and lounge in town, earning my keep, commuting to East Lansing Rapids to work with Dr. Reed on my degree and working on our musical. I was really separated from Nancy in distance wise and emotionally... I had my beautiful Siamese cat "Yum Yum" with me and Nancy had kept the other 'Black Balls." Unfortunately she went to the West Indies, left her cat with Karen who put the cat in a kennel. That was a sad day for the cat and a sad day for me. "Black Balls" died but I had 'Yum Yum" for nineteen years.

I was not only playing solo jobs and playing with some combos but was the pianist with a big band led by Ray Kuzniak. It seemed, so many times, the band leader was the <u>least</u> accomplished musician in the band. However he

176

was the one who got the jobs, had the charts and music stands. Ray Kuzniak was no exception. Tenor sax was his instrument and during his favorite solo, an arrangement of "Harlem Nocturne," we would await the usual moment when he' would skip beats. For a job in Petosky in northern Michigan, I was part of a jazz trio. The leader, black drummer Benny Carew, was the best and well-know drummer around. The bass player, Teddy Weatherford, was a swinging, short and chubby black guy with a moustache and really "got into it" when he played. It's not uncommon for the musicians to be invited, on heir breaks, to sit and chat with the guests at their tables and most club managers thought this was good for business. Not this manager! Benny and Teddy were told they weren't allowed to sit with the customers while I was. We were angry and upset.! "If you don't reconsider you won't have a piano player because I'll leave and you won't have a trio," I said. "They don't sit... I don't play!" The manager changed his mind and things went along quite smoothly after that. I must mention a few things here about Teddy, the excellent bass player. If ever I called him on the phone, no matter if weeks or months had passed, he would say, "Jack, we were just talking about you." Also, since he was bald, I learned later that he began wearing a "rug' as It's called. As he was walking from one room to another, on a job, it got it caught in a door.... Very embarrassing!

On the 28th of July I had my Doctoral oral exams at Michigan State. I was concerned sitting in the middle of a circle of professors who threw all kind of questions at me. For example: "How many symphonies did Brahms write and what were their keys?" "Who were "Les Six" and what did they write?" "Explain the overtone series and discuss Bach's 'Well Tempered Clavichord" "Discuss Schonberg and his twelve tone system," "Name Wagner's operas in his "Nibelung Ring" and their order." It seemed more like a history of music exam...easy questions and I PASSED! I had already taken passed from French exam, written exam and created the music charts. Now I only had to complete my dissertation orchestral work.

Afterwards June and Frank Miller and the Swets gave a party for me and I received my Ph.D. degree September 4, 1959.

(*I must remind myself and the reader that most of the information up to here has come from memory and the remainder with some help of yearly "At a Glance" type books I've written in*)

Around this time I received word that Nancy's father in Dearborn was very sick and in the hospital. Nancy would be flying home and wanted me to be there in Dearborn. After he came home from the hospital we left for New York and attended a friends wedding reception and an enjoyable experience seeing Robert Preston in "Music Man." However, while in New York I had a frightening experience!.

Having accumulated a few unpaid parking tickets while in New York, I went to court to settle and find out about the fines. I was brought before a judge who gave me a fine but I couldn't pay at that time. Next thing I knew I was behind bars for three hours. I was scared as hell, especially when someone came in to the cage

with handcuffs to take some the other prisoners
away. In the meantime, during a conversation
with the other inmates, they discovered I was a
Doctor (which I was) and began shouting threw
the bars: "Let 'em out, he's a Doctor. Let this guy
out!" It got the attention of a scared officer who
asked me if I really was. Of course I told him
"yes." He said "pay the damn tickets in the mail
and get the hell out" and practically threw me out
into the street!

When I returned to Grand Rapids Nancy
informed me that she was going to Georgia for a
quick divorce. She also had a new boy friend who
was the son of a well known newsman "Marcus
Childs." I sent her money and that was that! It
was sad but had to be! The year ended with Jack
the single man, "Concerto Grosso for Orchestra
and Wind Quintet" completed, a New Year's job
at Fifi's restaurant and most of all a Ph.D degree
in Composition from Michigan State University.
From now on and henceforth I was "Dr. Jack
Normain Kimmell."

Return to Grand Rapids and Summer Stock

I was now busy in Grand Rapids writing commercials by Adrian, for Kathy and me to sing for Gibson Refrigerators, performing once on the "Carol and Alex" Wood TV show teaching them dance steps which was pretty funny. I began again writing choral anthems for Beverly Howerton, Duncan Littlefair and the Fountain Street Church Choir. Besides playing jobs I was also doing some private teaching and was now quite involved with the church and hard at work with Adrian writing music for our new musical "Grass Green Sky Blue."

Somewhere at the end of the sixties I moved from the Swets house to my own apartment off a small street on a hill behind Fulton Street. My landlord was from some European country and could barely speak English. There were several apartments in the small building, others being occupied one time or another by American Indians or a gays. When I first moved in friends showed up one day with brushes and paint and painted the entire apartment for me. It turned out to be an apartment of great creativity and glorious entertainment which would take many pages to write about.

In the sixties I continued playing with Kuzniak, other groups, solo work and teaching. I became involved in so many things: giving a jazz lecture at Grand Rapids Junior College, becoming Musical Director of the Grand Rapids Civic Theater (my first show was "Kismet"), composing music for the play "Summer and Smoke" and later being hired as Musical Director for the Red Barn Theater in Saugatuck.

At the Civic Theater Mary Powell was wonderful in one of the leads in "Kismet." Although we were quite involved, she continued to be married to Bert Powell. I fortunately or unfortunately continued playing the "single man" game with several other ladies. (unmentioned here so as to protect the non-innocent.)

In November of 1961 I learned that the first movement of my Doctorial Thesis "Concerto Grosso For Orchestra and Wind Quintet had been
182

chosen to be part of a Contemporary Composers concert in Hartford at the Hartt School. The work had already won a thousand dollar award in the yearly national student composers BMI contest of 1957. I heard the concert and was quite thrilled hearing it for the first time as I walked into a rehearsal. One of the right-ups in the paper called it: "Concerto Grosso For Orchestra and Wild Quintet." *I never was quite sure whether that was a typo or not!*

I had become acquainted with a couple of "crazy" families around that time. The Richardsons and the Blankenburgs. Vicki Richardson was a thin little woman with glasses who reminded me somewhat of a younger Irene Ryan, the "Granny" on "Beverly Hillbilly's. She was constantly giving parties, including the Swets and I, and her rather farm-like house was like a halfway house for a rather strange brood of unusual people. The entire house was chaotic, especially her kitchen. Pots and pans and dishes were piled up and in complete disarray. But when dinner time came the most delicious dinner was somehow always on the table.. Vicki made me feel as though her place would always be a second home to me if I needed it. As for the Blankenbergs:

I spent some time with a young lady, Rita whom I'd met at the Theater. Rita was an excellent actress, a pretty, rather small naive young lady with bright blue eyes and sandy hair. She undoubtedly said her prayers every night for she was quite religious. One evening Rita and I were invited to the Blankenbergs for dinner and were welcomed into their fine house by rather tall, quiet, middle aged, reserved and immaculately dressed, dark haired Mr. Blankenberg. Ten or so minutes later down the stairs came Irene dressed (or undressed) in long black stockings and a "teddy," which is a combination of a tight sleeveless undergarment on the top (upper part of breasts exposed) and panties on the bottom. As Rita and I stood rather open-mouthed, Irene, noticing our surprise, didn't waste any time informing us they were "swingers" and hoped we were there to "swing," I began to stammer, Rita's face turned red and after softly muttering "oh my," she took me by the hand and yanked me out the door. Later I learned of the Kathy and Adrian Swets' Blankenbergs adventure. Out together for an evening dinner and in the middle of the meal, Irene suddenly disappeared under the table and headed for Adrian's somewhat spread legs. As she came up she said simply: "I was reaching for a star!" The Swets' and I never saw them but I heard that poor Mr. Blankenberg had been struck by lightning and killed.

I was at the Red Barn Theater in the summer playing the piano for "Gentlemen Prefer Blonds," beginning auditions for "Kismet" at the end of the summer and playing piano at a club "Loudons in the evening. "Kismet," with great music adapted from Borodin, opened in October of sixty-one and was a success with Mary playing the sexy part of "Lalume." I traveled with Adrain and Kathy to see several live shows at a theater in Detroit: "No Strings," "Sweet Charity" and "Bye Bye Birdie." That evening was especially memorable, not because of the show, but what happened afterwards.

It was a snowy night, we were returning and Kathy was driving my black VW Rabbit convertible between Lansing and Grand Rapids. I was in the passenger seat and Adrian had fallen asleep in the back. Kathy leaned over to light a cigarette, lost control of the car, ran off the road and overturned the car on its side sliding luckily in the snow. Adrian was thrown through the roof and his head was slightly cut. A passing car picked us up and took us back to a Lansing Hospital for a check up. Although we were all covered with bruises and my little VW was totaled and it was a miracle we all escaped without serious injury.

In the following summer I rehearsed "Music Man" at the Red Barn Theater during the day while I musically directed and played the unique show at the Civic Theater "The Fantasticks" in the evening. It was a fun as I played the piano and celeste on the stage as one of the characters.

Later in October I began rehearsals for Menotti's
186

opera, "Amahl and The Night Visitors" which was performed at the Civic Theater around Christmas time with Mary as the Mother. I had seen many TV performance of that opera but the performance of the "Mother" was never sung as beautifully as Mary's performance. Later we made a great recording of the opera with the cast (including a chorus), two oboes and me at the piano.

It was now around 1963 and I was commissioned to write spooky background music for the spooky play "Dracula" and began rehearsals for Frank Loesser's "The Most Happy Fella,," Mary played one of the leads and was terrific as the waitress singing several songs especially: "Oh My Feet, My Poor Poor Feet." I conducted a small orchestra to some great music. Soon Afterwards I was at work at the Red Barn with another Loesser show "How to Succeed in Business" and continually was writing music for our "Grass Green Sky Blue" Show. Then later came "Wonderful Town" at the Red Barn with

Mary as the lead, followed by "Guys and Dolls." Another adventure was about to take place!

On the last night of a show there's usually a cast party and on that night Mary's husband Bert had rented a cottage for a week or so in that summer for Mary and the family. Mary, being in the show had driven her car from the cottage to Saugatuck and the theater. Booze and food flowed plenty at the party and Mary certainly had more than her share of the booze, enough to make her stomach sick. Since it would be a drive back to her cottage, we thought it necessary for her to take some time to recover, which she did. Sick to her stomach, sitting in my car in the passenger seat with her head resting in my lap, suddenly "knock knock" on the window. And there was husband Bert! Quickly I rolled down the window and shouted: "It's not what you think! Mary drank too much and is very sick to her stomach."

Steaming, red faced Bert said, "Mary, get the hell in my car, NOW! I'll drive us to the cottage. Jack you take Mary's car and follow us!"

Following, I wondered what was going to happen next knowing that Bert had a rather lurid "past" that had landed him in prison and had come upon us in an awkward situation. After he dropped Mary off, Bert drove me back to pick up my car all the time threatening me with his lawyer.

Somehow I got around to discussing his job which was in the printing business. I made a deal for him to print a rather large amount of music manuscript paper for me. I still have much of the paper...a reminder of that precarious evening.

Adrian and I finally finished "Grass Green Sky Blue." I still had to write the orchestrations. It had its several weeks run at the Civic Theater in October during the 1963-64 season and was quite successful. Mary was wonderful in the female lead, most of the cast were great as far as acting. However I <u>was</u> disappointed with the two male leads. Paul Dreher, the director believed the acting was more important than the singing and I believed the opposite for a musical. Otherwise, I told him, it might just as well be a play. Being the director he won and I winced in the pit each time one of my songs was sung by one or the other the two male leads.

During those years, at the Civic Theater, I did "Kismet," "Grass Green Sky Blue," "The Fantastics," two productions of "Amahl and the Night Visitors," and "The Most Happy Fellow." At the Red Barn Theater I did "Sound of Music," "Music Man", "Camelot," "The Fantastics," "South Pacific," 'Guys and Dolls," and "Oliver Twist." I also wrote more music for the Civic Theater productions of Summer and Smoke," "Dracula," "Street Car Named Desire," and several other plays. I also played a lot of jazz with my group or others.

I continued having a number of female relationships during this period. Nothing changed! Married ladies or single it didn't seem to make much difference. I was humorously told it was an affliction and I played the piano and "all shucks" them into affection and "whatever." The strongest of my affections was for Mary which wasn't the smartest thing especially since she was married. But what the hell!? And being the musical director for musicals was an assist! My relationship with other women ended in disasters at that time. Mary was very hurt and never wanted to see me again. She divorced Bert and married Jack Stiles, quite well-healed, friend of President Jerry Ford and with whom Mary now had a wonderful new daughter Kathy. And Jack Kimmell was a stupid, self-center ass!

Richmond and Re-Saugatuck

The Director of Red Barn Theater in Saugatuck, Jimmy Dyas, was about to direct the musical Rogers and Hammerstein's "Oklahoma" at the spectacular Virginia Museum Theater in Richmond, Virginia and wanted me to join him as musical director. I packed and drove to Richmond and rented an apartment. The theater was wonderfully equipped and there was to be a fairly large orchestra. The musical was cast and was great, especially a lovely, very talented girl. Diana Goble, who played the roll of Annie and another girl who played the role of Laurey the lead female roll. Yes we became very friendly. The facilities for rehearsal were great as were the rehearsals, cast and orchestra who were members of the Richmond Symphony. The show was declared as the best ever at the theater and ran for several weeks. However, playing games outside, I had the misfortune of breaking a toe and had to wear a cast. When the show opened and the orchestra rose up from below on an elevated orchestra pit, I was in a special chair sitting with my toe

elevated, prepared to conduct. I was quite
coincidental that one of the viola players had been
at the Hartt School at the same time as me.
While in Richmond I was commissioned to write a
complete two piano arrangement for the Grand
Rapids Theater's performance of the Menotti
Opera "The Consul" of which Mary (now Stiles)
played the lead. I also was beginning an affair
with Diana and stayed in Richmond al little longer
while she did another dhow. I returned to the Red
Barn Theater with Jimmy, the director and Diana
to do the Sondheim Musical "A Funny Thing
Happened on the Way to the Forum." Diana was
going to do one of the main characters and I was
about to have a frightening experience! I was not
only the musical director but was talked into
doing the lead role of the Zero Mostel role
"Pseuolus."

Although I had been on the stage many
times as a kid dancing and later as a music
performer, it was never as an actor. Besides
difficulty remembering lines, I had to do the part
without glasses. Jimmy had me doing everything
193

on the stage he could think of and I "went up" a number of times on my lines. One time I forgot some of the lyrics and "scatted." Another time I was supposed to push one of two actors who both were dressed alike in women's clothing. I pushed the wrong one! I scared the hell out of the rest of the cast and certainly did the director....never again! The revue of the show said nothing whatsoever about my acting but did say they enjoyed the show but I was the only one who could sing.

The many shows I did at the Red Barn were great fun but hard work since we rehearsed one show during the day and performed different one in the evening. I played the score on the piano either alone or with another pianist we hired. When we did the show "Camelot," the leading man from New York didn't sing well enough to suit Jimmy. One of the songs he was supposed to sing off stage but Jimmy had me sing it on a mike at the piano. Summer Stock was always quite a wonderful, rewarding experience and after every show Jimmy and I stood outside and shook hands with the departing audience.

Return to the Big Apple and Mary Stiles

Diana and I decided to live together in New York. She was taller than me and was very strikingly lovely with long curly dark hair. She also was rather strange in many ways like not walking on grass with shoes for fear of hurting bugs and hardy saying a word when she was around a group of people. She was an exceptional animal lover and animals loved her. Every time we walked down a street dogs and cats came out from nowhere to follow her. Guys looked at me with kind of a sneer wondering what the hell I was doing with such a good looking woman and I think she cared about women as much as men but no matter what she was dynamite on the stage! We found a rather nice apartment on 73 rd Street on the West Side. The rear of our apartment building was next to the rear of the building called the "Dakotas" where later John Lennon lived and was shot. Diana played the piano and flute and was constantly searching the trade papers for actress work. She did fund work in several Off Broadway musicals and also traveled with shows to the Bahamas and Africa. In the meantime I was playing in clubs (I especially remember one night playing in a Club when I heard news of the assassination of Robert Kennedy). I was also arranging vocal recordings for two sisters and recording for a studio in Quincy a suburb of Boston. That was important because it was a great help financially.

The recording studio was owned by Ted Rosen a middle-aged money-making guy with a unique way of pulling in the cash. It worked like this: He advertised, for a fee, to record anyone's lyric to music. That music was a number of background music recordings he had bought, including several from me. They were all types, religious, country, pop...you name it and I had them pretty well memorized. The lyrics were almost all extremely amateurish; even some I could hardly read. I was given an envelope of fifteen of them at a time, looked over each in a hurry and made a selection of which recorded music I thought would fit. Then I gave it to the studio recording technician... zoom, one right after another. Each finished recording was recorded on a phonograph record and sold to the client.

Because I had such a good feeling for melody and rhythm, without any rehearsal, I was able to sing each lyric and made it fit the recording exactly. I still have a number consolidated on old twelve inch records and imagine I'm probably the most recorded vocalist in the whole wide world!

During those times I also began an association as the pianist and arranger for Tito Mora a Spanish baritone. Tito was a good looking, talented Spanish guy with a beautiful voice who had much fame in Spain, won many awards and came to America hoping for the same kind of fame. In the early 70's I did all his arrangements and traveled with him for engagements at a wonderful club in Birmingham, Alabama, the Fontainbleu Hotel in Miami Beach (in a room where Sinatra had performed) and another club in New Jersey on the ocean. We also appeared on the Merv Griffen Show and I wrote and directed a record album for him "Tito Mora, Ven A Mi." which included several originals of my lyrics and music.

198

Tito wasn't haven't the success he wanted and was used to so he headed back to Spain. I've heard from a few times throughout the years and read somewhere where he had given up a liver to a needy patient.

I had always been am Indy 500 race fan since I was a kid and heard the cars zooming around the track on the radio. I knew all about A.J. Foyt, Mario Andretti, the Unsers, others and the English drivers. I finally decided to travel to Indianapolis and see and hear a race. I had an agent in New York who was able to book me at a club in Indiana at race time so I stayed at the Swets' and drove to Indianapolis several times for a race. One year the race was rained out so I had to sleep in the car. The next day it was rained out again so I had to leave and miss the race completely that year. It turned out to be a sad year because when the race was finally run a driver was killed in a terrible accident. I was never much of a drinker but a friend once suggested I try 150 proof rum. When I was booked again at a club, during race time, a gentleman wanted to buy me a drink so I ordered 150 proof rum. Years later, when Mary and I were playing at the Hyatt Regency Hotel in Phoenix, the waitress suddenly brought me up a glass of 150 rum. I was very surprised and asked how and where it came from. She pointed a man out to me and it was the same gentleman!. I must have made an impression on him. Weird!

Another time when I was visiting my best friends Kathy and Adrian in Grand Rapids they were having a party and of course Mary, who still married to Jack Stiles, was there. As she was about to leave I leaned over to kiss her. "No way," she said in a VERY determined voice. Since Diana was always away each time she returned we were more convinced it was not to be so we finally split up and I found her another apartment. I don't know what happened to her or if she might have changed her name or married but I've always hoped for her success because she was one talented actress.

I visited Grand Rapids again for a concert I'd arranged for Tito and this time a serious romance began again for Mary and me…especially since she was unhappy in her third marriage and was separated. At the time I never knew, besides her theater performances, that she was a famous lady. That is until I learned of the famous "Grand Rapids City Hall Tower" event.

In 1969 The city of Grand Rapids was going through an "Urban Renewal" chapter and among the things to be destroyed was the old classical Grand Rapids City Hall. Much of the city were up in arms about what was to take place. Mary's husband, several others and Mary were the leaders. As it was about to come down, Mary handcuffed herself to the wrecking ball, her picture was taken and it appeared in newspapers all over the world and in magazines. Mary was the famous "woman on the wrecking ball" and the woman, this time I intended to mary Mary!

The events leading up to our marriage were extremely complicated and somewhat vague in sequence involving: trips back and forth between New York, Grand Rapids, Bloomsburg and Massachusetts, court proceedings, a rental cottage on Cape Cod, threats by Mary's husband over custody of Kathy, Mary's near fatal pulmonary embolism and hospital stay. And it all took place around the time of the Watergate trials in the very early 70's. Since any more detail of these events may not be of great interest to the reader, I will leave it at that for now.

While I was in New York in the early 70's I received a call from the Grand Rapids Symphony. They were about to do a production of Andrew Lloyd Webber's "Jesus Christ Superstar and would have a sold out audience, but suddenly they received notice the authority for outside production had been revoked. No music! There was hardly any time but, "could I take the necessary orchestral music off a recording?" I said I would try. I began immediately and as soon as they sent me a plane ticket I was on my way, still writing while on the plane. Upon arrival at the concert hall I continued writing and giving pages to copyists to copy and hand out to the orchestra who quickly rehearsed. It was a panic but we made it in time for the concert.

202

Soon afterwards a Jazz-Rock group called "Kenny Gordon and the Sound Gathering" commissioned me to write a jazz production arrangement of "Jesus Christ Super Star" to have a run at a large Motel in Grand Rapids. It was a talented musical group with great musicians who not only played but sang, including an excellent female singer and Kenny himself. I came back and conducted. It was a great success, ran for many nights and was later taken on the road and to Canada. I remember one of the performances clearly because it was the first and only time I ever smoked a marijuana cigarette. Before the performance I was coaxed into trying one. During part of the performance, I suddenly turned around and began to conduct the audience!

Because I had been commuting to Ted Rosen's studio in Massachusetts, I moved out of my New York apartment in September of '73., found and rented a house at 38 Surfside Rd. in North Scituate, with a small lake behind and moved in. It was a lovely location right across the street from the ocean and somewhat near the Minot Lighthouse. I thought it to be a pretty good sized house but when Mary's furniture arrived I could hardly find enough space to sit down. Soon afterwards, when she had mostly recovered from her illness, I flew out and Mary, Kathy (getting sick on the Peace Bridge) and I drove back to North Situate and settled in arriving around the beginning of November, '73.

This was a period of time when we worked together playing two piano jobs around Boston, lugging around a sound system and electric piano through snow, good weather and bad weather. (Mary was playing their acoustic piano and we were both singing my arrangements). Along with the Ted Rosen caper we were doing okay and often had visits from several of our wonderful Grand Rapids friends. Like the time, one late night, when friend Joanne and her male friend Jerry came to visit us. Suddenly, as we were sleeping in our bed room on the second floor at night, there was a loud "bang!" Our rope bed our guests were sleeping on, had crashed to the floor with them in it. We all "broke up!" It was assumed a particular kind of action was the cause.!

As before stated, Mary's husband Jack Stiles claimed that since we weren't married, he would take Kathy away from us. We intended to get married eventually but <u>now</u> was the time. However there was no way we were going to tell Mr. Stiles! We contacted a justice of the peace who would notify us of the time. When it came I was at the hardware store with Kathy who I'd promised an ice cream cone. Mary's call to the store, " Hurry the hell home quick! They're here to marry us." We tore home (Kathy whining because of no ice cream) and Mary, still quite not recovered, lay in bed. As I sat on the bed too, the rather frail looking older Justice of the Peace and his lady witness (both right out of a movie) pronounced us man and wife on my birthday, Dec. 8, 1973. Mary and I laughed about it later because, although it was a strange scene for us, it seemed a perfectly everyday occurrence for them. The words "I do ("or will") were wonderful to speak and hear over the sound of the ocean! (It's important to mention that Kathy and Mary were great horse lovers and Kathy has always owned a horse, but "Slopey," who was now with us, belonged to Mary.)

In 1974 we decided to move and found a wonderful house to rent at 29 Lamberts Lane in Cohasset, not far from Scituate. It was large with several stories and newly built in a rustic style with boards with square nails. The bedroom had a fireplace and was large enough for our king size bed and a ping pong table. We loved the rather secluded and quiet location and enjoyed an English couple neighbor and the horse barn we had constructed. (I didn't know exactly what I was doing but I made the barn window) Also Mary's Mimi and Mike stayed with us at times.

Somewhere during this period of time Adrian Swets and I were commissioned, through the Fountain Street Church in Grand Rapids, to write an approximate hour long choral work for the choir. Adrian got to work on it and sent me, week to week, the libretto as I composed the music. It was named "Magic in the Heart of the Universe," in ten sections. It's basically was about ones life from infancy to old age and written also for percussion, organ, piano and flutes. I flew to Grand Rapids to final rehearse and conduct its first performance. Afterwards, with staging by Paul Dreher and added choreography, it was first performed October 9th of 1975 at the Grand Rapids Civic Theater. A representative from the well known publishing house Shawnee Press, who had already published choral works of mine, came to the opening and decided to publish it. It's been performed many times locally and throughout the country. One of the sections: "Winter Comes" has become quite popular especially for Memorial Services.

Around 1976, while n New York, Adrian informed me that the Saint Cecelia Music Center was having a bicentennial song contest and if he wrote words would I write the music. He sent the words to me, I wrote the music and we won the contest receiving a moderate sum of money. Also Dr. Reed commissioned me to compose a jazz work for the Michigan State University twenty or so piece Jazz Orchestra. I wrote a fairly long work called "Cohasset Summer," flew out to East Lansing with Mary and conducted the performance. (I recomposed the work later for the Grand Rapids Symphony and also conducted).

In 1976 in April we learned that Kathy's father, Jack Stiles, was killed in an automobile accident in Grand Rapids. Since Mary and Jack were divorced, Kathy traveled to Washington frequently to visit Jack who was an assistant to President Ford. She could have been with him that evening! It was a sad day when Kathy came from school and we had to tell her.

While living in Cohasset, Kathy and Mary days and hours were filled with carting Kathy and her horse in her trailer to jumping and dressage events throughout New England. The walls of her room were filled with ribbons she'd won. It was a wonderful time for both, and Mary and I were very proud of her. (Throughout the years Kathy has had a number of different horses.) Kathy's inheritance from her father's Trust was a big help at that time and the following years. While in Cohasset we did have the pleasure of becoming friends with two English couples.

Welcome to Arizona

One day our landlord notified us he was selling the house. We had first choice but decided it wasn't quite what we wanted and "to hell with this New England weather!" We decided on Arizona and "Scottsdale here I come." Off I went looking for work and since we had worked the Radisson Hotel in New England, I was able to land us a job at the local Radisson. I also rented us a house with a flat roof that later leaked in a big rain storm. (When Adrian and Kathy came to visit at Thanksgiving time, Adrian and I were on top of the roof shuffling off rain.)

Later we bought a wonderful house on East Paradise Drive with a swimming pool and large area in back, behind a wall, where we had a Porta barn built. It was a paradise! We enjoyed having a swimming pool except it was lots of work keeping it clean and loaded with the proper chemicals. It also seemed, so many times, as soon as I finished cleaning it, a dust storm would come along and dirty the damn pool all up!

We finished at the Raddison and began a five year run at the Phoenix Hyatt Regency Hotel in the 80's under the name "Kimmell and MacLean" with many vocal arrangements I'd written and a "Unit" (rug) on my head! *(Idea courtesy if our jackass agent.)* I also began teaching some music classes at Scottsdale College, South Moutain and Phoenix Junior College.

The Hyatt is 24 stories and right across the street from Symphony Hall with a restaurant that slowly goes round and round on the top floor. By this time Mary had switched from stand-up bass to the electric bass and was a great player. We performed six nights in the Plaza Bar on the Atrium and watched the elevators go up and down. It was very enjoyable except for having to haul our sound system out of a closet every evening.

Recalling my concerning my "unit"….. One evening an Indian convention filled the Atrium, Indians, some with feathers and Indian outfits. One of them started toward us, probably to ask for a request. As he was about to approach I said to Mary (pointing to my "rug," Maybe I should just give him this and get it over with." We performed there for fifteen seasons and didn't enjoy it so much near the end when the food and beverage manager we liked so much left. Here is a typical remark by the new manager: A busy convention was on the Atrium restaurant eating and drinking and the manager glides over to us and says, "Don't play anything slow so they'll drink more."

We met lots of great people there, one in particular whose name was Hamm. Lucky for me there was a Indy race track right outside of Phoenix and a highlight for me was to buy a VIP ticket which entitles me to food and beverage in a tent and great seats for the race. Larry Hamm was an insurance man who partially owned a race car. And his driver for the race was Lee (I can't remember his name but he was well known). Larry was my kind of pal! He took me into the pits and introduced me a bunch of race drivers, especially his driver Lee (can't think of his name).

I wrote kind of a country song for Larry called "Battlin' Lee and Larry got me on a conference call and I played and sang the song for a bunch of the drivers over the phone. Somewhere around this time I was beginning to write chorus arrangements for Janet Sessions and her Phoenix Singers and a number of two piano arrangements for Sue Whittaker. We enjoyed our property and had a solar heater installed on our roof as was common in Arizona. But two incidents arose that were pain in the butt.

First a bunch of large houses were to be built next door in the large empty property. Since there was supposed to be a small path with entrance to our horse section we were about to be shut out. We raised hell with the city and they not only took care of the entrance on the side but built us a gate.

Mary had warned the city about possible flooding because of all the new houses being built but to no avail. One day there was a terrible rain storm and water flooded our pool and pool system, horse section and almost into our house.

Mary went to bat at a meeting with the city managers and we were reimbursed for damages and had a wall built around our property. I was ignorant about all the stuff but Mary had plenty of experience from her Grand Rapids day.

YEAAAAAA Mary! By the way we had a sweet dog at that time "Magic" and a close friend Kay Lyon, Kay's friend Thelma, and Mike Karish who began as our handy man and became our dear friend. *(His father was mentioned earlier in the "rattlesnake story)*. I also had some eye and chin surgery done around that time but it never made me better looking!

I was having, off and on, great fun jobs at Sun City West playing piano with a fairly large orchestra for well-known entertainers such as Carol Lawrence (of West Side Story), Shirley Jones of musicals fame, Morey Amsterdam (Dick Van Dyke show), Charo (female singer with Cugat),the Lennon Sisters, Impersonator Rich Little, Tennessee Ernie Ford and others. The theater was huge and packed the musicians excellent, the rehearsals short and the money good.

I was hired to be musical director at the Phoenix Theater and did a number of shows including "They're Playing Our Song, Fiddler on the Roof,"etc.(this is all in 1982-83). My "dad" was also in the hospital at this time. Good times and bad times during this time and one of the bad times was our Kathy's breaking her jaw

Events which I remember, but would just as soon forget, were Mary and my engagement with the Victor Lombardo band at the fames Arizona Biltmore Hotel. Victor had been one of the "shaky vibratoish" sax players with his brother's famous "Guy Lombardo's Orchestra but one could hardly find a more pain in the ass band leader than Victor no matter the search. Not only was he a miserable musician but he was plain stupid! We were supposed to be featured with the band but were given one song each to sing. Mine was "Feelings" which I hated. Once, during a tune when I was "filling" on the piano I was given hell and told not to. Soon after when I thought, "I'd

better not" he said, "why aren't you filling"?
Typical! He and I fought all the time and finally I
said, "Victor, you might not be the worse
musician I've ever met but you're certainly in the
top five." We later had some "name" acts appear
and after a rehearsal with Victor, the act was
desperate and came to me to take over which I
did from then on. Once he turned to me, as and
was about to go on, and said, "Who's that?" Mary
and I couldn't stand it and quit and learned later
he had been fired for loud arguing with someone
one or other. All the while Mary and I were
performing at country clubs, bars, restaurants,
private parties...you name it with some help from
our agent Chuck Eddy.

*(I must remember to mention that we
always have had cats....one Siamese "Yum Yum")
for 19 years and a beautiful little black one "Girl"
for 19 more years and many dogs. As I write now
we have the best pet ever, our wonderful sweet,
beautiful, athletic, intelligent, sensitive, part
shepherd and part collie "Willow.")*

In September of '84 Bob's wife Velma died from a heart attack. I had written some things here about her earlier. At the time Bob and Velma had been separated.

In December of 85 we began a thirteen season at the unique, expensive, highly rated Rockefeller owned Boulders Resort a few mile north of Scottsdale. It was a beautiful night-clubish room with appreciative and wealthy audiences for whom I wrote book loads of solo and duo voice arrangements which included past and present musicals. The Boulders Resort was the best, our kind of job around and the best we ever had.

In April 1985 my "dad' died I and flew to Bloomsburg. The ceremony was disappointing because the Minister spoke of God more than my dad and afterwards I gave him hell. Because of my mother's failing health, the family properties and wealth were put in the hands of a Bank Trust under the direction of a Mr. Boop who was kind of a 'boop." It all began to become very complicated and unravel.

At first I couldn't understand what was happening because mother was now beginning to show signs of early Alzheimer's, doing and imagining strange things ... like people coming to rob her. I came to realize there were serious problems when she began putting everything on her desk into her large purse, including the telephone. Twenty four hour ladies were hired to be with mother and at first Bob was controlling things with the Trust. (The Trust took over completely when it seemed hae ws spending money for personal reasons.) She did have a chance to come, with one of the ladies to visit us, and it was very sad and distressing. Finally she was taken to a hospital in Hershy, Pa in 1928.

I was commissioned by a wonderful alto sax virtuoso, Hugo Loewenstern from Amarillo Texas, to write an album for him and a computerized small orchestra. It was suggested I stay at his house in Amarillo in July of '85. He also got me a job at a Country Club and later at the Sheraton Hotel. I sort of moved in with the family, in my apartment upstairs and we all and Mary have
218

become life-long friends. It was a wonderful time, playing on a boat, staying at their cottage and arranging and composing for a great musician! I finished and was away for 92 days. The recording session took place later in beautiful Sedona.

Mary and I were back at the Boulders. We met many great people there but two we especially liked. They were a fun wealthy lawyer and lovely who came every evening to hear us and drink champagne…. partly because every evening, smoking his big cigar, he came up and sang the "Java Jive." ("I love coffee, I love Tea…a cup a cup a cup, a cup!")

(Somewhere in all this life style it was discovered I had a hernia and according to my records had an operation on Thursday, the 21st of September, 1986.)

On January 29, 1988 my mother died in Hershey, Pa. from problems caused by Alzheimer's. Mary and I travelled to Pa. for the funeral and it was all very sad except for something that could only happen to me.

I was still wearing my "rug" and was getting ready to come to the funeral. Mary had already gone with Bob and some other people. In the process of trying to get the damn thing on I got the sticky stuff that holds it on all over my fingers. When I was about to drive my fingers stuck to the door and then the steering wheel. While everyone was waiting for me I was searching all over Bloomsburg for someplace to get the sticky stuff off. I finally did, arrived at the funeral, told my story and "broke" everyone up. My mother would have laughed too!

The properties and finances, in the hands of Mr. Boop and the bank, since there were no other relatives involved, had to be divided between my brother and me. I never dreamed they had been so wealthy and they certainly didn't live like it but they did work their tails off accumulating it. I wasn't about to enter any partnership with my brother so he got the properties and I got the money! Mary had been to Europe with her sister Suzy several times but it was time for me to finally go now that I could afford it. So it was off to Europe for us both!

Europe

Sue, Mary's sister, and Mary had travelled and explored and Scotland then returned to London. Sue went home to Arkansas and I flew to London to meet Mary where I was so tired I had to take a nap. In the evening Mary and I did some exploring and later went to a theater to see a Webber Musical that was all on roller skates, "Starlight Express." We both weren't too crazy about it but it helped us to remember London before we headed to where we really wanted to go: Paris in September, 1988.

We flew to Paris and stayed at a fine hotel not far from the Eifel Tower. We had breakfasts in our rooms, went up in the Tower to view Paris, explored the Louvre (we never thought the Mona Lisa painting was so small), the Notre Dame Cathedral, the Picasso exhibits, Montmartre...the upper section of Paris, boated on the Seine River, to name a few of our activities. I followed Mary everywhere and she even seemed to know the shortcuts. I was a bit frustrated, when at times, I wanted to speak French to the French, the French wanted to speak English to me. I loved most every minute of the trip, in spite of being aware we were sometimes being overcharged in cafes because we were American and having to pay extra for cream in coffee. Mary did remind me often that I coped out on seeing a dirty show in one of the nasty theaters. We also took a train and visited Versailles where Mary thought she lost her watch (it had crawled way up on her arm.) We couldn't believe the heights of the rooms, the artistry, the mirrors, the richness, the mammoth halls. I think Mary's most favorite moment at Versailles might have been when she had to pea in the gardens. Now if we can just get our asses to Rome some day!

Home, Owen and Stuff

Living in Scottsdale had some special advantages. Folks liked to come visit like: my Nephew Kevin from California, Mary's sister Susie from Arkansas, Adrian and Kathy Swets from Michigan, my mother and brother from Pa., Dr. Reed and Mary from Michigan, Mary's son Chuck from(?), Mary's niece Betsy and husband John, etc. etc. *(I must include some things here about Dr. H. Owen Reed and Mary his wife Mary.)*

Went I first new Owen he was married to a very nice, very proper, highly educated, somewhat haughty lady. She died a number of years after we met and he remarried a woman, named Mary, who was a number of years younger than Owen. Mary, in many ways, is the direct opposite from his former wife. Although being very smart, she's somewhat uneducated, not up on the styles of today, loving and dedicated to Owen, somewhat raunchy and a hell of a lot of fun! The first day they came to our house in Scottsdale, they arrived in a van that looked like its last owner was a Rock Band. In the evening we had a bedroom all prepared for them but Owen said they'd sleep in the van. His words were, "If the van's a rockin,' don't come a-knockin'! Owen also enjoyed sending me funny limericks he wrote, many of them pretty raunchy. Both were great fun when we visited their home in Michigan near a lake or later in Green Valley near the Mexican border in Arizona. The last time I saw Owen was the evening the Blue Lake Fine Arts Music camp in Michigan Camp gave a concert of his music before a huge outdoor audience a few years ago. I sat in the front row next to him and during the program Owen (who was then in his nineties) was helped up the stairs by his daughters, sat down at the piano with a fine jazz group and played one of his favorite songs "Here's That Rainy Day." When he came to sit down he hugged me. Owen Reed wrote one of the most performed contemporary choral pieces in the repertoire for chorus: "Michigan Morn" and for band: "La Fieta Mexicana." The last time we spoke on the phone he was 101 old.

The year 1998 ended our job at the Boulders and was sort of a disaster year for me because I was diagnosed with Prostate Cancer. It couldn't have been more complicated but after I had various treatments to consider, it was decided I would have an extended five days a week radiation treatment which ended July 14, at a wonderfully equipped new Mayo Clinic in Scottsdale not far from home. Being zapped by a big machine in my gut was pretty painless at the time but caused some future side effects including fatigue. Everyone was wonderful to me and I sort of repaid by playing a grand piano for other waiting patients when I came for treatments. Wednesday, May 20, 1998 was a day for me that will "last in infamy!" It was also a bad time for our wonderful little black cat "Girl" who was diagnosed with kidney problems. But I never stopped composing and performing, writing many choral and instrumental works, especially for trumpet and trombone which were being published and writing poems for Mary on: Mother's Day, Christmas, Birthday, Marriage

Anniversary, Valentine's Day, Easter and endless numbers for other people and other subjects.

Since, sometime ago I had written an album for Hugo, we decided that it was time to make a good recording so I travelled to Sedona, a beautiful red-rocked town north of Phoenix. I had recorded most of the orchestration on Finale and stayed for several days recording with Hugo and his daughter, including some original compositions. It had its ups and downs but turned out very good. About this time I wrote a Wind Quintet in three movements which I much later recomposed and added a fourth. It was also around this time (1999) we decided to sell our wonderful property. (Michigan called and won!).

Re-Grand Rapids and more Composing

After several "almosts" in November, we sold the house and were on our way back to Grand Rapids in our big Van. NOT AGAIN!!! Mary had gone ahead and found a new house and there we were with all our belongings on Kirkwall Drive.

(During all this time, Kathy's money from her father's Trust had helped us a great deal financially. She had moved away, gotten married and divorced, had more horses, been to Europe, stayed with us off and on but was still the most important other member of our family).

We enjoyed the house, and the big yard (much to take care of) in back especially after Adrian had it painted and soon after moving in I was commissioned to write background music for the Civic Theater play "The Uninvited." The music and lighting were the only good parts of the half-ass play! We became members of the Fountain Street Church but it was never the same after Duncan Littlefair and was going through financial trauma with its Minister and its finances. It was also the beginning of Mary's "Kitchen Ladies:"

Mary, Kathy Swets, Carolyn Hines and Joanne McElwee and my music teaching at Aquinas College and its subsidiary Emeritus. I didn't realize the students were so ignorant of past music. One day I was mentioning George Gershwin of who most had never heard. I had to remind them that if they ever had to call United for a flight, the music in the background would be Gershwin's famous "Rhapsody In Blue." Part of my commitment was also giving musical talks at various other venues like "Retirement Centers." I enjoyed it all! It was a time we even joined a book club. (Believe it or not, I was still writing music for Ted Rosen in Quincy.) I was also recording and did a concert with Dave Miller and his group and getting to know Mary's son Mike and his wife Joanie and two children Mike and Rebecca and sometimes seeing Mary's daughter Mimi.

I joined the Beltline Big Band in 2001, as a pianist singer, and all together wrote around 120 arrangements, including originals and tunes for me to sing. It was a pretty good big band of four trumpets, four trombones, five saxes and rhythms section owned by a lawyer, Marilyn Tyree and her husband Steve. Some of it was great fun, consider low or most no pay, and some was a pain in the butt which I won't go into. It lasted until 2013 when Steve died and we played many jobs, including the annual Festival downtown, and recorded several albums that included "That 'Ol Jack Magic" which were my arrangements and dedicated to me. Mary and I also became great friends with Fred and Ruth Moen who, along with the Swets,' were a great part of our lives.

Our Kathy had long since graduated from Arizona State with honors in Bachelor and Masters degrees, had worked as a telephone therapist, then trained and became a Flight Attendant for United Airlines. Then along came "9/11." It not only changed most everyone else's life, but changed Kathy's and ours.

Because of the attack on the towers, all commercial planes were grounded. So Kathy, who was working the flight and Colin Hatsell, one of the pilots of their plane, were stuck in St.

Louis. They'd never met before but Kathy rented a car to come home and Colin hitched a ride as far as Chicago where he was based. Although it was a frightful day in America it had a wonderful ending for the two of them. They fell in love, later married and Colin became our wonderful son in law. It's hard to believe but four weeks later a special Jewish gentleman, Don Herman, came to me for piano lessons and still does! Besides teaching I was still playing lots of club jobs here, there and everywhere, many with Mary and always writing for FS Church and arranging for someone or other. Because of my gift of inheritance I'd invested, I wasn't worrying too much. Once when Mary and I played a job at the Grand Rapids Museum, her picture on the wrecking ball was on the wall right across from us.

It was a fun experience in 2002 when Paul Dreher asked me to music direct a show "Inside Out" at the Wealthy Theater. It was an all-women show and besides being music director, I played the show on piano with Mary on bass and a drummer. The show ran for four performances and the last night was very snowy. We thought there wouldn't be much of an audience but our biggest crowd of the run showed up.

Soon after that a sad day for us was when our sick sweet little kitty "Girl," we'd had for nineteen years was put to sleep. It seemed so many times we had lost a precious much loved pet! A good day for us at the time was when met two of our very best and favorite friends, Jill and Jim Marrese. I also became a member of the Jazz Society Board….. Lucky me! By the way I had a car I liked for quite a while. My Nisson I saw I'd seen in a window in Arizona and bought. Betsy's John drove it up for me to Grand Rapids.

I was still connected to Fountain Street Church and some of my favorite evenings were when Adrian and I went to Duncan Littlefair's house with other folks, in the evening, for an extensive talk ritual. We were still having visits from Susie but felt they were getting far in between because of her attachment to our house in Arizona.

Because of a new pipe organ at Fountain Street Church I was commissioned to write a large work for organ and chorus to be performed by a renowned organist Carlo Curley. As I was writing the words for chorus in the third the movement, I repeated some of them to two of the gentlemen involved in the commissioning. Since Fountain Street Church is an extremely liberal church they said: "You can't use the word "God" in the choral words. I disagreed and picked up the phone and called Duncan and repeated their criticism. "BULLSHIT" he shouted. I kept them in!

My organ piece "Exaltation" was performed (not as well as I would have liked) and I was proud of it. The commission didn't pay enough for the work but "what the hell!!!" I was commissioned the write words to the "Vision words" at FSC and did but the words were all out of sync and I had it performed for a smaller group. I also wrote a funny birth song with Adrian for Duncan.

The sad: It was around this time that Kathy's most favorite horse "Midnight' died. The good: Mary sang a great song "I'm Still Here" from "Follies" in a show at the Circle Theater. I thought she was the best! In the meantime, our large yard in the back is too much work and we're too far from everything, including hospitals so let's sell the house!. We did and bought a Condo in what I called "Condoville." It was a hell of a nice condo if you like condos! It's location was great, closer to town and everything else. We moved in October of 3003. Not too big and not too small and nice but I don't like my music sounding like anyone else's and I don't like my house looking like every ones else's. Here we go again! But another big moment came on December of 2003. Kathy found the perfect dog for us in Lansing and Willow came into our lives!

The New Year's (2004) most important event was in April when we attended Kathy and Colin's wedding in St. Augustine, Florida. The service was on the beach by the ocean down from a cottage they'd rented and was beautiful and cute when their doggie had the ring on him. They moved to San Carlos, California and Kathy resigned from United, and decided to become a cop. After the police academy she became a police woman in San Carlos until they decided to come more east and move closer to us. They chose Holland, Michigan.

Mary had begun to expand her horizons when she began art classes and began to paint wonderful paintings. It was a pretty good year right up until Bush was reelected in November. I wrote down "BOO!" then and I'll write BOO! Now! On July 20, 2005, my brother Bob died and on page eight through ten I've already written much information.

I was, as usual writing much music, including a rewrite of the eighth section of "Magic," for an upcoming concert, many more arrangements for the BB Band including an original "Misty Moon," more music for Hugo, "God Is Love," a piece for Cello and Piano, and "Paul's Piece" which I wrote because of the death of Jim Marrese's son Paul and music for Pat Dermody.

Mary and I also travelled up to the tip of Michigan for a concert with Eileen Serafis and Dan

Jacobs. It was a great day in December of 2005, for our dear friend Jim Marrese, who was Canadian, to become an American citizen after much persuasion from us. I will also mention that at times I've had precancerous skin problems have had had Mohs surgery in 2006 and several times and it ain't no fun! Our dear friend Debby Swets husband, Jack Slater, died in 2006 and it has always affected her life very much since.

This might be a good place to mention something important that may belong earlier in this chapter. In 1984 the Grand Rapids Symphony Orchestra performed, in concert, my composition, "Cohasset Summer," which is a large orchestral work that includes some Jazz instruments. Adding to the honor of this event is the fact that I was the conductor.

Family and Grand Children

The biggest events, which happened in 2006, were the arrival of pictures of our Kathy and Colin's new adopted beautiful baby Sophia from China and their trip to Hong Kong for their baby. I also wrote a song for them and recorded "Lullaby for Sophia." It wasn't too much longer that Kathy and Colin went away, this time to Korea, where they adopted a sweet baby boy they named Keenan.

The following year one of our closest and best friends, Adrian Swets had been sick sometime with Alzheimer's and was slowly fading. It was so sad to see and realize such a wonderful, intelligent and creative man was slowly going downhill! Also our other dear friend, Fred Moen, recently suffered a heart attack. Fred was terribly overweight and I tried many, seemingly hopeless, ways to help him lose weight. This (2007) was also a time when Mary was very ill and was in the hospital several times until it was found she was suffering from "Giardia" a sickening stomach ailment which, fortunately she was cured. It was also at this time that Fred dropped dead, in his bathroom, of a heart attack and Mary's sister Susie died. We even sprung a leak in our waterbed. This was definitely turning out not to be "A Very Good Year!" One good thing , I began a long run playing piano on Tuesday mornings at the Lions Club and it was the beginning of this "memory trip." We spent this year's Christmas in Holland but both and I ended the year 2007 being sick. Hell of a way to end a year! And a few days later I had a colonoscopy...OUCH and U We still have our old GMC Vantura Van but gone is my wonderful Nissan. We did buy a brand new greyish 2007 Honda Fit that year from Riverside Honda and it's a peach!

Willow got skunked by a skunk in early 2008d we . ke writing band arrangements for the band and others and playing at the Lions Club, especially for a very special gentleman Clarence Anderson who enjoyed pulling up his chair close to the piano and guessing the tunes.

In May of 2008 our best friend, Kathy Swets' husband Adrian died. He had been in the

Veteran's Home then later in Clark's Home. It certainly was the end of an era for all of us. Our dear friends, Jim and Jill Marrese, who'd lived down the street, sold their Condo and bout a residence in Florida. They also had a house built in Traverse City. It was a great disappointed for us but we're glad it was good for them. Thank goodness we had Willow to help buoy up our spirits. Since Fred Moen had died we were spending much time with Ruth Moen as she had become a dear friend, especially for Mary and a great enjoyment. But, since we had invested in the stock market we weren't enjoying those ups and downs.

The most important music I was working on was recomposing my wind quintet (over and over, (will I ever be satisfied?). It was decided I would write a Cabaret for Mary, MacAdam and me to be called "Everything Must Change." It was to be much fun, much work, some arguing, and much rehearsal. I wrote a number of original songs, including the lyrics, and we used others already written that fit. Marnie and Mary both sang, Mary

played the electric bass and I played the piano
and sang. The show lasted about an hour. We had
our first performance (rehearsal) at Kathy Swets'
condo for an invited audience and seemed to be
enjoyed. "Everything Must Change" was
performed a number of times at different venues,
including the Grand Rapids Circle Theater. I made
changes from time to time and it was always very
well received. In 2008 I also recomposed music,
written at another time, for the Civic Theater's
production of "Summer and Smoke" and recorded
the orchestra on Finale. It was lots of work but
ok. But in the production, some of the music was
faded out pretty quickly and there went my notes.
Woosh! Mary started the new year of 2009 in
Hawaii, a particular place where I never really had
any desire to go. Beautiful mountains and
volcanos and forests and lakes and other assorted
awesome scenes of nature were never high on my
priority for travel. Give me cities like Paris and
Rome and Cairo and New York and Rio and
Athens and assorted sky lines and I'm your man!

Our Cabaret, and the BB Band and assorted jobs were keeping us busy and I was still playing at the Lions Club, but our dear friend Ruth Moen was back in the hospital with cancer again (we thought she was doing fine) and she died in August of 2009. It was a real emotional trauma, especially for Mary. During the last number of years we had lost my mother and dad, my brother Bob, Mary's mother and father, Mary's sister Sue, Adrian Swets, Marinus Swets, and Fred and Ruth Moen. The glories of a senor citizenship! It did give us an opportunity to become friends with the Moen's son John and his family who were now owners of the wonderful Moen's cottage by Lake Michigan. Kenny Gordon, from the "Superstar" arrangement was after me again to do some other musical project on speculation but this time "no thanks."

The BB Band was still going strong, my numbers of arrangements written were probably getting close to a hundred and my singing voice was still pretty good *(I'm often told it's still so good it's "freaky").* But my ears weren't so good for now I had to purchase hearing aids and that certainly was a big change in my life. It was especially awful because, when I played the piano it sounded like somewhat beating on tin, a kind of instrument no one would ever want.

Things by this time were very complicated for our Kathy and Colin. Colin had been furloughed from United Airlines and was hired by a Japanese airline (Nippon Airlines) Because of Colin's complicated flying connections; they decided to move to Arizona. Kathy was now here searching for a house to buy and it was heart breaking for us, especially Mary, because Sophia and Keenan. They moved in July of 2010 and now would be far away again in Anthem, Arizona, a northern suburb of Phoenix.

At least my piano soloing would be enjoyable for me and those who enjoyed jazz piano. I was hired to begin a monthly piano concert at the Grand Rapids Art Museum on a wonderful Steinway in an acoustically great large hall. Not only that I bought a large TV for Mary's birthday.

Years before, after the success of "Magic," Adrian wanted to write the libretto for another musical and had written much material about a "Junk Man." I found it and rewrote it as a large poetic work that might be set to music. It was never finished and sits in a cabinet with stacks of my musical compositions and arrangements performed and not performed. But I was in the process of re writing and composing dialogue and one of the movements of "magic" even though it was published. It was going to be performed in a concert again at Fountain Street Church on April of 2011.

Mary, in the meantime, was having serious bladder problems and was in contact with appointments at the excellent Univ. of Michigan Hospital in Ann Arbor and our "darling niece" Betsy was diagnosed with breast cancer and was undergoing treatment in Colorado.

It was also, at this time and this year (2010) that I met a great guy Walter Lockwood who asked me to compose music for a musical. I worked on it consistently for several months and into the next year, composing the entire score which was to be called, "A Thousand Bad Pianos" and mostly took place in a Retirement Center. Later Demos were recorded, including my singing and piano and it was submitted to the Grand Rapids Actors Theater but was turned down because of the complexity of the script. I was told that the music was well liked. It sits on my computer waiting for who knows what but is another big time consuming disappointment.

As the new year arrived some events were Mary's cataract eye surgery, my recomposing my "Ballade for Oboe, English horn and Piano" and rewriting some of "Magic" for an upcoming concert. The "Ballade' was performed in California by Althea Waites and her group and was later published by "Imagine Music." This year I was beginning a long period of not feeling too strong, feeling groggy and sometimes weak. And no one, including doctors, seemed to know why. It's still hanging on as I type this. Because I didn't pass my eye exam for driver's license I had to have a cataract operation on my left eye. Things I couldn't see without glasses I can now see and with close up things I have to wear another pair. I took the test again and passed. Lucky me, bad eyes and bad ears. Just what a musician prays for!

I did have some inspiration from our wonderful friend Jill Marrese. In Florida she took up the bassoon and inspired me to write "Five Duets for Bassoon and Piano."

Also Mary and I had been attending a book club which tried to meet once a month. We read a bunch of books and lost a lot of members either through demise or lack of interest or age problems. Oh....this wonderful senior citizens'! And most times when you get on the phone and it's medical or government or programming or write, etc. they ask you your age which is none of their damn business! There's got to be a better way to find out if you're who you say you are! I wrote a couple poems about that and age. Here they are and you'd better laugh or at least snicker:

Birthdays (June, 1991)

Your birthday's a day to remind you you're born
I know that each time I wake up in the morn
And each time it happens I say, "I'm still here!"
Then I hear "Happy Birthday my dear."

People don't say, "hey kid, whadaya like?
Would you rather be president or ride on your
bike?'
No they say, "Hey kid, how old are you?"
A question that sticks forever like glue.

It's "sweet sixteen" first and then twenty one
They measure your life and spoil your fun
When one day you're told you've reached
middle age
Each paper you're on has your age on its page.

They print in the news "mugged by guy twenty
eight"
I sure don't care 'long as jail is his fate
They print this man died, "he was fifty seven"

Never mind what his age, did he get into
heaven?

Dogs Buster and Milo don't have our age in their
folder
They don't care if we're twelve or forty or older
Who cares if you're sixty or still a young pup
As long as you're healthy and can still get it up.!

I'm speaking my piece, you know how I feel
When it comes to my age, well it's mine to
conceal
But just try to keep it somewhere in obscurity
I'm told now's the time for my social security.

I'm incensed by this perpetual reminder of age
This "senior citizen" stuff is a total outrage
Got things on your mind and weight on your
shoulder
They give you a party and remind you you're
older!

I used to think I could choose any age
To your mother, my brother, to them age is
the "rage"

I love them and honor all their curiosity
But not when it comes to my birthday and
me!

You think that I'm crazy, it affects me too deep
And Sue and even you call me "the little creep"
Ok I'll give in. some restraint I'll display
I'll wish you my love a HAPPY BIRTHDAY

The Golden Years (April, 2007)

It's fun to be a genuine senior citizen
Don't mind all those wrinkles in my face
I feel so much closer to myself
When every vein in my hand I can trace.

It's fun to be a genuine senior citizen
Senior benefits galore for me and you
Our senior maturity brings social security
Along with all that Medicare Blue.

We're "senior" listed on the backs of menus
Though portions they claim aren't quite as large

And movie theaters treat us extra special
A generous saving off the price they usually
charge.

If at times it's difficult to hear the dialogue
When you watch that movie at the Mall
Don't fret about the plot or all the action
Just take someone who's young to explain it
all.

We're privileged to be genuine senior citizens
No more tests for jobs or tests at some old school
The tests we take are now just pleasant visits
To some Lab to test our brain or blood or stool.

I just love being a genuine senior citizen
And the challenge to remember this or that
And to know there'll always be someone
somewhere
To remind me where I've been or where I'm at.

I know this dame, a complaining lame senior citizen
Who's habitually a loud unhappy talker
But she's quiet now and happy as can be

'Cause she has this brand new delux folding walker.

It's satisfying to be a genuine senior citizen
If your life seems down and love has lost its clout
Just ask your friendly doctor for some samples
Of viagra to straighten all those problems out.

You may have travelled all around the world
Stayed at lavish hotels Paris, Bankok or Rome
But maybe comes the day they won't compare
To that welcome lavish "Home Sweet Nursing
Home."

It's a joy to know I'm in my "golden years"
Makes my days and charms and warms my heart
It's so good to know I'm part of something special
'Stead of just some raging, aging, gray old fart!

"Magic in the Heart of the Universe" was performed at Fountain Street Memorial Concert in May of 2011 the same day my "Ballade of Oboe, English horn and Piano" was being performed in California. Soon after I sent a recording of the "Ballade' to my publisher "Imagine Music Publishing" and it was later published in 2013. This was also the year (since we had a water bed) we had the "water-bed Caper" trying to secure a new one from the company because of a leak which we did. But it was a big pain in the ass! It was much easier having our bedroom painted and with new carpet. I also sent a Latin piece for band I wrote called "Mambo's Mambo" named after Kathy's horse. It was published by Triplo Press later.

Walt Lockwood talked me into writing another musical with him called "Don't Get Married." I wasn't very enthused about it not only because of the subject matter but because of "A Thousand Bad Pianos" that wasn't performed. However I wrote twelve or thirteen new pieces that sit there staring at me from time to time.

Dr. Jack Normain Kimmell

A strange thing happened in March of 2013.
I had been writing back and forth to an old Hartt
School mate Alice Micalarous (Aliki) and she sent
me an old letter which stated that I had a check
coming from a musician recording session in New
York in the fifties which I'd never received. After
exploration and phone calls and writing to New
York State I finally received a check for one
hundred and forty some dollars. What a strange
event!

I was still playing solo piano at the Gram
and piano at the Lion's Club on Tuesdays but
since the death of Steve Tyree, husband of band
owner Marylyn, the Beltline Big Band was shut
down which in some ways was Ok since Marilyn
was always much fun and my hearing was
gradually getting worse. Also in April I was having
all kinds of physical problems: Hot flashes at
night, losing weight (approx.12 lbs), fatigue.
Generally not feeling too hot!

My good friend Don Herman was still taking
piano lessons and we kidded about "our people."
(my being Jewish somewhat Jewish). This was

252

also a time when the former director of the Civic Theater, Paul Dreher, of whom Mary and I did many shows with, died of cancer. It was a very sad time!

In July 03 of 2013 was the "Mary's sleep machine" event which didn't do so well at the cost of some money and a number of phone calls. Around this time I signed a contract for my "Expression for Flute and Piano" and my "Duets for Bassoon and Piano" was published. The biggest and strangest happening of the year was when Kathy and Colin and Sophia and Keenan, who had been living in Japan, left Japan and moved to Guam. (Where the hell is Guam?") Colin had been flying for a Japanese Airline but was now back flying for United Airlines.

It was in October (2014) that our Kathy swallowed some food the wrong way and seriously had to be taken the two Guam Hospitals (where she was badly diagnosed). Thank god Colin later took a hospital in Honolulu which actually saved her life. The entire event her remaining in the hospital for a time and was

wonderfully helped by "our darling niece" Betsy,"
husband John (in Hawaii at the time) and Colin
who was magnificent. It was all very scary and
improbable and strange and we were all
concerned she might be lost to us. Kathy is now
in the process of recovery.

While this was happening far away, Ed
Clifford, a wonderful musician and the Grand
Rapids Art Museum gave a Sunday concert of
some of my compositions on Sunday, October
27th, 2013. It included:

Expression for Flute and Piano
Five Duets for Bassoon and Piano
Enigma for Cello and Piano (performed Martha
Bowman)
Excursion for Alto Sax and Piano
(all of these accompanied on piano by Mary Lou
Smith.)

Three vocals:
"When I Think of The Things" from "Grass Green
Sky Blue"

"Molly's Song" from "Don't Get Married"

"Fifth Wheel Baby" from Cabaret:

"Everything Must Change"

and: Kimmell piano improvisation from audience phone number.

The concert was very crowded, the audience was very enthusiastic, with standing ovation, and the musicians, including longtime friend and pianist Mary Low Smith were especially wonderful! This might be a good time to mention my published music at this time and Musicals I've served as Musical Director.

MUSIC PUBLICATIONS

Five Duets for Bassoon and Piano, Ballade for Oboe, English horn and Piano, Mambo's Mambo (for Band), Flourish from Nine Celebratory Fanfares for Six Trumpets, Oratorio and Stage Musical: Magic in The Heat of the Universe, It is Good, This is What We Are, Glory to God, Blessed Miracles, God is Love and All Good Things, Consider the Lilies, Grand Rapid Grand, Suite for Four Trumpets, Suite No.2 for Four Trumpets, Suite of Short Pieces for Brass Septet, Scherzino for Trumpets, Dyad for Horn and Piano, Quartet in Four Movements for Four Trombones, Con Lenezza for Four Bb Trumpets, Enigma for Alto Sax and Piano, Expression for Flute and Piano, Three Intradas for Three Trumpets and Piano, Duet for Flute and Piano.

MUSICALS DIRECTED

Fiddler on the Roof (2 times), Amahl and the Night Visitors (2 times), Most Happy Fella, Grass Green Sky Blue (original), Magic in the Heat of the Universe.. Choral Work and Musical (original), Fantastiks (3 times,(Grand Rapids Civic Theater,

Harrisburg Theater, Red Barn Summer Theater), Camelot, Guys and Dolls, South Pacific, Sound of Music, They're Playing Our Song, Oliver, English Title, Kismet, Inside Out, On the Town, A Funny Thing Happened on the Way to the Forum, My Fair Lady, Wonderful Town, How To Succeed in Business, Unsinkable Molly Brown, Boy Friend, Music Man, King and I, Oklahoma, Gentlemen Prefer Blondes, Dark of the Moon.

MUSIC COMPOSED FOR PLAYS
Dracula (2), Summer and Smoke (2), Old Wicked Songs, Streetcar Named Desire, The Innocents, Merchant of Venice, The Lark, Romance In D, Menotti's Opera "The Consul" (arranged for two pianos), Indside Out (arranged for rhythm trio), Cabaret: Everything Must Change (both composed some music and arranged some)

At the beginning of November Kathy was released from the hospital in Honolulu and returned to Guam and Mary left for Honolulu November 17th. This was about the time I began having unexplainable nose bleeds have continued once and awhile, but I was still performing solo at the GRAM and the Lions Club, and composed a trumpet piece, "Intrada for Three Trumpets and Piano" which is to be published by Triplo Press. At this time we were saying goodbye to 2013 and hello to 2014.

I've been thinking about it off and on, especially since I've had very little communication with any of my relatives recently except Kevin, LouAnna and DonnaJean...only Mary's. Let me think: My blood relations are: Nephew Kevin, Bob and Graig (and his children), Nieces Donna Jean (and her children), and LuAana *and her children), only remember one on my mother's side (was a Mayor) and Gladys (my mother's sister's daughter. My relations have been mostly with those on Mary's side: John and Betsy Hennesy, Carol and Glen, Hoss (on the phone).

This "Memoir" has not been edited for mistake's, etc and is being concluded in March 2015. Material has not been entered for some time as of March.

My life, as it had been, ended on Sunday, in February, 2015, in the morning, when my precious talented, beautiful, wonderful and loving wife, Mary Kimmell, had a serious stroke in our kitchen, falling against the refrigerator. I called 911 and she was immediately transported to Blodgett hospital. She was later transferred to Mary Free Bed and later to where she is now in room 203, Porter Hills to hopefully recover. Kay Lyons and Kathy and Colin Hatsell, (with son Keenan and daughter Sophia) have been here in Grand Rapids, helping me with all care for Mary. I would be (and probably will be) practically helpless and 'a Zombie" without them, their necessary care, love and concern, attention to details (financially and all others)... then, now and into the future. Mary has had cards, caring visits, flowers an love from many friends who love her.

I hope for some bright rays of sunshine in the future but don't have the mental capacity and ability to continue this "Memoir." So am concluding as of today, Friday morning, March 6^h, 2015. I sent this file to Fed Ex Office of Grand Rapids and have printed several copies for those who would ever want to care or interested to read these personal memories. I will be shortly on my way to visit Mary at Porter Hills, Room 203 or wherever else there she may be for rehab. Best wishes, thanks and love to all.

[Note: Ben Swets asked Jack for a chance to submit this manuscript to be printed at Amazon in March 2017.]

--- *March 2017*

Dr. Jack Normain Kimmell (born December in Colorado Springs, Colorado now residing in Grand Rapids, MI) ...husband of and forever, with my love for my precious, talented, kind, caring late wife Mary Stiles Kimmell.

Made in the USA
Lexington, KY
28 August 2017